CAMBRIDGE

Official Cambridge Exam Preparation

CB081777

5

Power Up

Pupil's Book

Colin Sage

With Caroline Nixon and Michael Tomlinson

Map of the book

1 In style

1

2

3

4

5

6

7

8

9

Which clothes can you see in the pictures?
When are the clothes used?

Watch the video. What does Jenny use as a scarf?

Mission Write a review

1. Choose an activity and make a shopping list.
2. Design an online clothes shop. Then swap shops and go shopping.
3. Write a review of the shop.

1 1.02 **Listen and point to the clothes. Then match the clothes (1–11) to the words in the box.**

handbag	jumper	raincoat	suit	swimming costume	tie	tights	tracksuit	trainers	jewellery	blouse

SEARCH

I love looking at clothes online, and here are some of my favourites. I'd love to get some of them one day … and it's my birthday soon!

1

You can put your phone in this.

2

Great for riding my bike in the park.

3

I ♥ this. It's warm and cosy!

4

You'll love ☂ if you wear this coat.

+ make new board

5

Something for my brother (if he ever gets married?!?)

6

This is beautiful – but more $ than some cars!

7

My geography teacher wears this! It's awesome!!!!

8

My favourite tennis player wears these!

9

This is perfect to wear in spring.

10

These are cute! And they look really comfortable.

11

This is more beautiful than a sunny day at the beach 🕶.

2 In pairs, read the sentences. Are they true for you?

My teacher's wearing jewellery.

No, she isn't.

My teacher's wearing jewellery.
I've got a handbag at home.
I've got a swimming costume.
My teacher often wears a tie.
There's a raincoat in my bag.
I'm wearing a jumper.
My mum's got a tracksuit.
I'm wearing black tights.
I've got a yellow blouse.
There are trainers in my bag.
My dad's got a blue suit.

3 1.03 **PRONUNCIATION Listen and repeat.** page 118

1 Read Jim's blog and answer the questions.

1 What did Jim and Jenny want?

2 What were the problems with the things they bought?

3 What is a shopping fail?

Jim's Big Blog

Online Shopping Fails

22nd March @12:25 pm

Last week, I bought a T-shirt online to wear at my friend's birthday party. I found a few websites where you can write on T-shirts. On one site, the T-shirts weren't as expensive as on other sites, and they looked nicer too. My friend is learning Spanish with me so I asked for 'Happy Birthday' in Spanish on the T-shirt.

The T-shirt arrived more slowly than I hoped. In fact, it arrived a few minutes before my friend's party. I put it on as quickly as I could then I left to go to the party. The T-shirt felt great – it wasn't bigger or smaller than I wanted.

When I arrived, I showed the T-shirt to my friend and he started laughing. I was confused – but then he told me about the problem with my T-shirt. It didn't say 'Feliz cumpleaños' on the back. It said, 'Happy Birthday in Spanish'!

At first, I was angry – but my friend said that the T-shirt made him happy on his birthday. Then I felt a lot better.

SHOPPING FAIL

22nd March @12:45 pm

Last month, I made an online shopping mistake that was as bad as Jim's.

My feet are growing quickly so I needed a bigger pair of trainers for tennis club. I looked at two different websites. On the first site, the shoes were much more expensive. But on the second site I saw a pair of shoes I loved – they were bright red and they were very cheap.

My mum ordered the trainers for me but when they arrived I was surprised. The box was very small. Then, when I opened the box, I was shocked. The trainers were a lot smaller than my feet. And they were smaller than my toes too! In fact, they were trainers for a doll! What a mistake!

Now, I always check the size of the things I buy online.

2 Read the blog again. Who says each sentence – Jim or Jenny?

1 'My old ones are too small.'

I think Jenny says this.

2 'Great! I love the colour and they're not expensive.'

3 'Wow! This is really comfortable.'

4 'This is awful! I look so silly.'

5 'That's strange. Why's this so small?'

6 'I'm happy it made you laugh.'

Grammar look: comparative adjectives, adverbs and *as … as*

'The trainers were a lot smaller than my feet.'

'On the first site, the shoes were much more expensive.'

'Last month, I made an online-shopping mistake that was as bad as Jim's.'

1 What is bigger? **the trainers / Jenny's feet**

2 Where did the shoes cost more? **on the first site / on the second site**

3 Whose mistake was worse? **Jim's / they were similar**

4 With short adjectives (one or two syllables long), we make comparisons with *-er than / more … than.*

5 With long adjectives (three or more syllables long), we make comparisons with *-er than / more … than.*

6 We use *as … as* to say something is the same or **similar / different** to something else. For example: 'I took the T-shirt out of the box as quickly as I could.'

7 We use *not as … as* to say something is **similar / different** to (and usually less than) something else. For example: 'The T-shirts weren't as expensive as on other sites.'

page 120

1 **Make sentences to compare the pictures.**

The tracksuit isn't as old as the trousers.

Did you know?

In the 1860s, some dresses were as wide as doors. Women often got stuck when they walked between rooms!

Mission Stage 1

Choose an activity and make a shopping list.

Hiking
a warm jumper, a cosy hat, trainers, a raincoat, trousers

1 1.05 **Match the sentences (1–7) to the clothes (A–G). Then listen and check.**

It's got gold buttons.

The dress.

1 It's made of **cotton.** It's got a picture of the sun on it.

2 It's made of **leather.** It looks good for cold weather.

3 It's got a blue **collar** and it's made of **silk.** It's got gold **buttons,** too.

4 It's got a parrot **pattern.** You wear it round your neck.

5 There's a small **size** and a large **size.** You use them when you go walking.

6 It's got long **sleeves** and it's got a price **label.** It costs £25.

7 It's got a **chain.** There's a crocodile on it, too.

2 ☆ **In pairs, talk about what you like wearing at the weekend.**

3 1.06 **Listen to Safi and Rav packing.** Do they need winter or summer clothes?

EXAM TIP! Write times as numbers (for example, **12:15**) not words (for example, quarter past twelve).

4 1.07 ☆ **Listen again. Complete the timetable.**

School trip timetable

Tuesday:	Airport bus leaves at: **(1)** 6:15
Flight:	10 am–9 pm
Wednesday:	go to the **(2)** ______
Thursday morning:	shopping
afternoon:	**(3)** ______ at the hotel
Friday:	go **(4)** ______
Saturday:	whale watching at **(5)** ______

Grammar look: the present simple with future meaning

When does the bus leave?

At 6:15!

1 What tense is the question? **present simple / *going to* future**

2 What time is the question talking about? **the present / the future**

3 The present simple is used to talk about timetables (for example, for buses, for lessons at school or for a holiday) in the **future / past**.

page 120

1 Put the words in order.

1 flight / When / does / leave? / the

____

2 Where / start? / does / the / trip

____

3 does / tour / Where / the / finish?

____

4 is / time / dinner? / What

____

5 the / day / What / party? / is

____

2 **Choose one of the school trips.** Ask and answer the questions from Activity 1.

1

2

3

Mission Stage 2

Design an online clothes shop. Then swap shops and go shopping.

1 **Look at the pictures. Which sentences do you think are true?** Read and check.

- The story is about a king. ______
- The king's servants help him with everything. ______
- The king goes swimming one day. ______
- The king finds a fish in the sea. ______

1.08

King Canute's day on the beach

I am a servant to the great King Canute. He is a good and powerful king who can do anything. My friend says that she saw him climb the castle as fast as a spider! And my dad told me that he can swim to the bottom of the sea to talk to jellyfish.

This morning, the king was sitting at the breakfast table, looking at the fish on his gold plate. 'Oh dear,' he said, 'I just want fruit for breakfast today!'

'Oh no!' I thought. 'I'm so sorry, your majesty,' I said. I immediately picked up the fish and someone brought a bowl of fruit that was as big as the table! 'I will do whatever you want. You are our good and powerful king,' I said. 'Thank you,' the king said, but he looked annoyed. 'People always say things like that to me, but I don't like it!' After breakfast, the king went to his bedroom to get dressed. I took his silk shirt, suit and best leather shoes from the wardrobe. His cloak and crown were on his bed. 'Oh dear,' said King Canute in a loud, angry voice. 'I just wanted to wear comfortable trousers, a shirt and boots.' I rushed in with the clothes the king wanted. 'I'm so sorry, your majesty. You are our good and powerful king.'

Again, the king looked annoyed. 'People always say things like that to me!' he complained. 'Why does everyone always, always say "yes" to me?' 'Because you're the king, your majesty,' I replied. I helped him with the buttons on his cotton shirt and I didn't say anything else.

Suddenly the king said, 'I want to go to the beach and I want everyone to come with me. Bring my throne.'

Soon everyone was at the beach. 'So … I am a powerful king. Everyone has to obey me,' said the king. 'Does the sea have to obey me?' he asked. 'Of course,' we all replied. Then King Canute sat down on his throne at the edge of the water. He shouted to the sea, 'I am your powerful king! You have to obey me. Don't get me wet!'

I couldn't believe what I was seeing! I was excited to watch the sea stop completely. But then, something strange happened. The sea didn't listen and the tide came in. First, the water covered his boots. Then his trousers and his shirt! The other servants and I stood there with our mouths open. When the sea was as high as his shoulders, King Canute stood up and we all ran to help him.

When we were all back at the beach, the king turned to us and said, 'You see, I am very wet. I am your king but I don't have superpowers. I can't control the sea. The sea doesn't obey me. So, stop always saying "yes" to me. It's very boring!'

2 In pairs, talk about the questions.

1. Do you think King Canute is a good person or a bad person?
2. What doesn't the king like about his servants?
3. Why does the king feel frustrated? What does he do to solve the problem?
4. Imagine you are a servant. What would you say to the king after what happened at the beach?

1 Look at the pictures and answer the questions.

1. When did people wear these clothes?
2. What do you think the clothes are made of?
3. Which styles do you like the best?

2 1.09 Listen and read the text. What clothes can you find?

3 Read the text again and say *yes* or *no*.

1. Everyone could wear silk in the Middle Ages.
2. Cotton is a manmade textile.
3. You need 25 plastic bottles to make a fleece.
4. Fleece is better for the planet than wool.
5. Smart textiles can change shape.

4 In pairs, talk about the questions.

1. Which materials is your shirt made of?
2. How do you think we will use smart textiles in the future?

Clothes in the past

In the past people used natural materials to make their clothes like animal fur and skin. They also used leaves and plants. In the Middle Ages, most people wore warm woollen clothes which came from sheep. Shoes were very simple and they were made of leather. Only very rich people could wear silk and colourful clothes, as dyed fabrics were expensive.

What we wear today

Today, we still use many natural materials for our clothes like cotton, wool, silk and leather. We also use manmade textiles, like acrylic, polyester and nylon. People like them because they are cheaper than natural textiles. They have different qualities too – swimwear is made of manmade materials because they dry faster. Our clothes often have both natural and manmade materials. Check the label on your T-shirt!

Fleece is a very special, manmade fabric. It's made from recycled plastic bottles. You need 25 plastic bottles to make a fleece sweater or a blanket! Fleece fabric keeps us warm, it's waterproof and it helps us to look after the planet.

What will we wear in the future?

In the future, we could all be wearing smart textiles. These clothes have little sensors hidden inside and they catch energy from our body. They can change colour, light up and even grow. Smart textiles are important for sport. For example, a T-shirt could help keep a football player cool during a match. Smart textiles can also be fun. Imagine your friends' faces when your T-shirt changes colour at a party!

Did you know?

In Europe in the Middle Ages, they didn't make shoes for the left and right feet.

1 Match the text types in the box to the examples A–D.

a short email	a note
an advert	a notice

EXAM TIP! Think about **where** you would see each message. What sort of words do you use in those places?

A

B

Sara,

Don't wash your clothes in the washing machine. It broke this morning. You can use the sink in the kitchen.

See you later,

Mum

C

IMPORTANT NOTICE

PLEASE TAKE OFF YOUR SHOES BEFORE YOU ENTER SECURITY

D

Dear Bill,

We change your towels daily and clean your room every morning after breakfast.

We hope you have a great time!

Janet Mills

(Manager)

2 Look at the texts again. Match the titles (1–4) to the texts (A–D).

1 Hotel information ______

2 A machine that doesn't work ______

3 Airport information C

4 A special offer ______

3 Read the text and answer the questions.

George,

Uncle Bob will be here for dinner tonight. Please buy him a nice birthday present after your lessons. He loves funny ties!

Dad

1 What kind of text is it?

______

2 Who wrote the message?

______

3 What does George need to do?

______

4 When should George look for a present?

A at dinner time

B before school

C after school

______

1 1.10 **Listen and match.** Put the pictures in the correct order.

I've marked your test and I've got some good news!

That's E.

A

B

E

C

D

2 1.11 **Read the questions and look at the pictures.** Which words will you hear? Listen and check.

1 Why can't Karen help her mum?

A
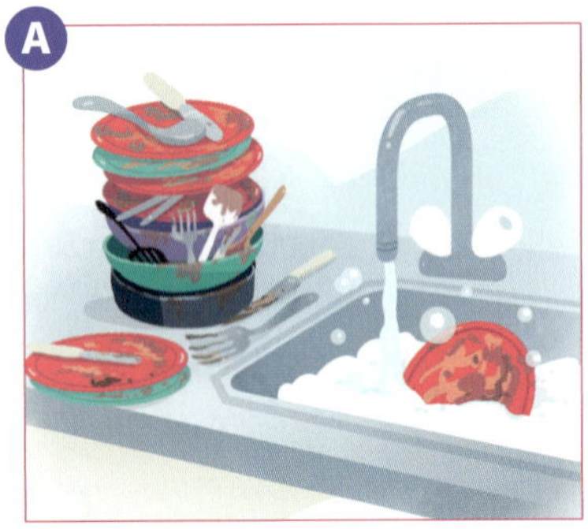

B
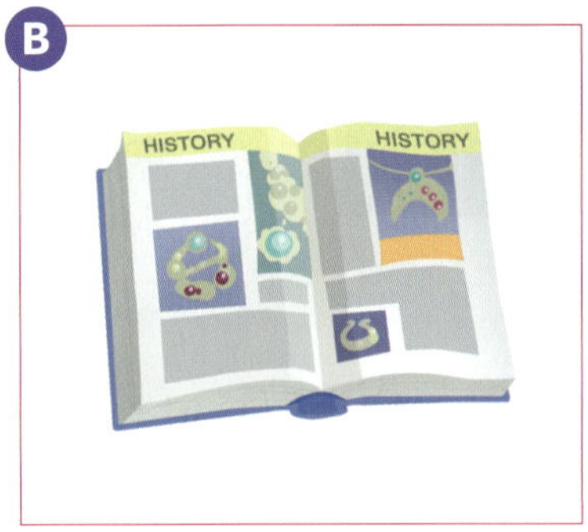

C

2 Which trainers does the boy take?

A

B
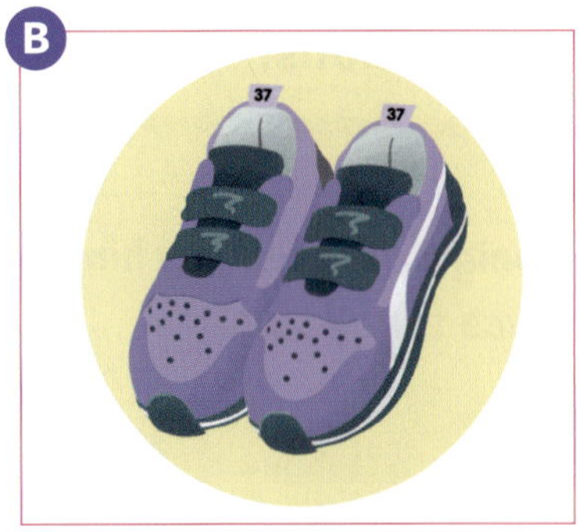

C
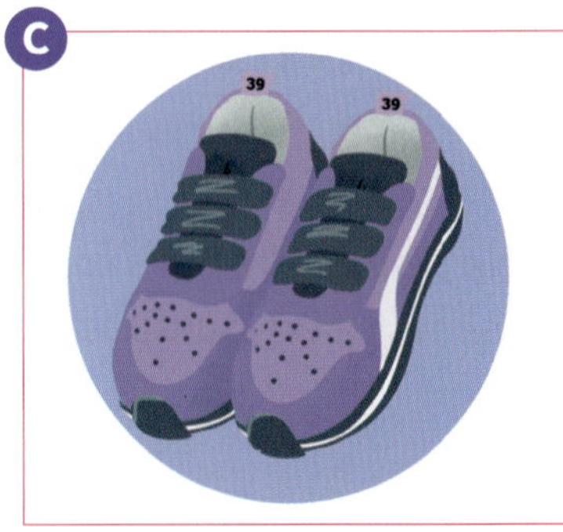

3 1.12 **Listen again and choose the correct answer.** Why is this correct?

EXAM TIP! Use the **first** listening to choose an answer. You can check your answer the **second** time you listen.

1 Complete the sentences.

1 My jumper is old, but my tracksuit is older.
My jumper is newer *than my tracksuit*.

2 The red raincoat is expensive, but the blue one is more expensive.
The blue raincoat is more ________.

3 My raincoat is smart and so is my suit.
My raincoat is as ________.

4 My cotton socks are comfortable and so are my silk ones.
My cotton socks are as ________.

5 My old jumper is big, but my new jumper is bigger.
My old jumper is smaller ________.

2 Complete the sentences. Use the correct form of the words in the box.

finish	open	leave	start	close	arrive

1 When does the toy shop ________ again?
At 9 am tomorrow.

2 When does the bus ________ ?
In fifteen minutes.

3 What time does the film ________ ?
At 12:30.

4 The school ________ after lunch on Saturday.

5 The concert doesn't ________ until 8 pm.

6 The train ________ in two hours.

3 Choose ten words from this unit. Record the words using the steps below.

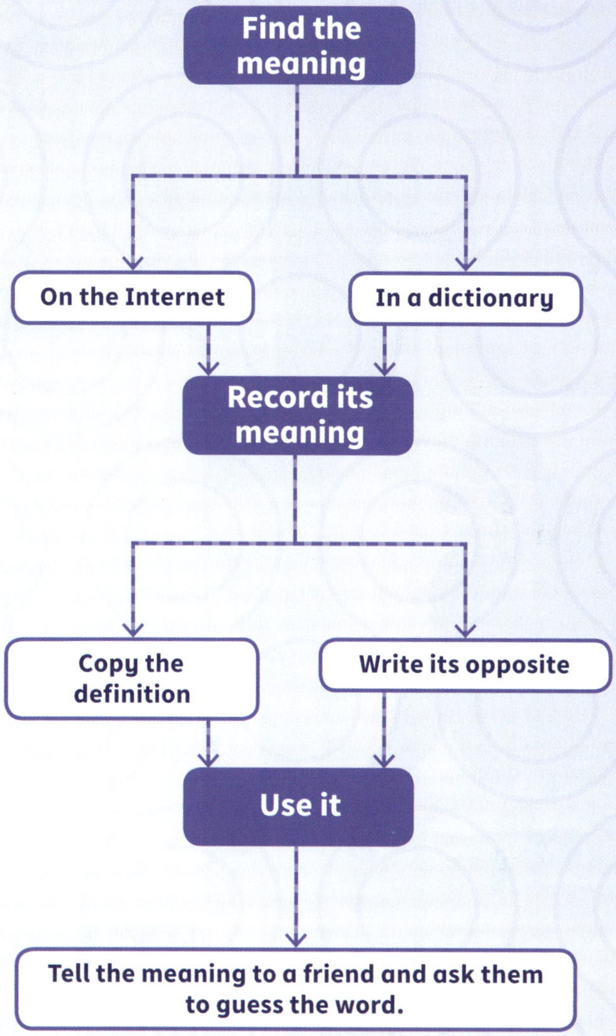

Mission in action!

- Say what activity you had to buy clothes for.
- Say why you chose the shop.
- Write a review of the shop.

The silk blouse was the correct size and colour. The order arrived in perfect condition. I can recommend this online shop for smart clothes. ★★★★★

2 Future technology

1

2

3

4

5

6

7

8

9

Is the technology in each picture useful? Why? Which would you like to use the most?

Watch the video. Why does Jenny need to clean Jim's earphones?

Mission Recommend new technology

1. Find the class's technological needs.
2. Show how a piece of technology works.

★ Present your group's best option.

1 1.13 **Listen, point and say the numbers.**

This is my laptop. I use it …

Number 4.

2 Match the words in the box to the numbers 1–10 in the picture.

software disc hardware laptop
screen mouse printer
computer program keyboard mobile phone

Number 8 is software.

3 Look at the words in Activity 2 and complete the challenges.

1 Find the six kinds of hardware.
2 Write a sentence that uses the words 'disc' and 'program'.
3 Find three things that turn on and off.
4 Name three pieces of computer software.

1 **Look at the poster.** What can you see? What would you like to look at?

Look! There's a robot dog.

2 1.14 **Listen to Tom talking to a friend about a technology show.** What's the address of the show's website?

____

3 1.15 **Listen again.** Match the people (1–5) to the objects (A–H).

1 ☐ 
Sarah

2 ☐ 
Dale

3 ☐ 
Brian

4 ☐ 
Courtney

5 ☐ 
Scott

A 
mobile phones

B 
laptop

C 
keyboards

D 
screen

E 
digital printer

F 
mouse

G 
software

H 
robot dog

4 1.16 **PRONUNCIATION** **Listen and repeat.**

page 118

EXAM TIP! Remember that there are **three options** that aren't used.

Grammar look: the first conditional

'If my mum says it's OK, then I'll go.'

1 Will Sarah's mum say it's OK? **Yes** / **Maybe**

2 We use the first conditional to talk about things that **might** / **won't** happen.

page 120

1 Which sentence is correct? Choose A or B.

1 **A** If my mum says it's OK, I'm going to the park this weekend.
  B If my mum says it's OK, I'll plant some tomatoes tonight.

2 **A** I get a new hat if it's not too expensive.
  B I'll buy a new keyboard if it's not too expensive.

3 **A** I'll have fun if I join the school basketball club.
  B I'll have fun if I'll play video games tonight.

4 **A** Kim will email her aunt if she finishes her homework in time.
  B Courtney goes too if she finishes her homework in time.

5 **A** If I go to the fair, I'll see all my friends.
  B I go to the school disco, I'll see all my friends.

6 **A** If I go to the fair, I'll look at the robots.
  B If it rains, have to stay inside.

2 Complete the sentences. Use your own ideas.

1 If my mum says it's OK, ________ .
2 ________ if it's not too expensive.
3 I'll have fun if ________ .
4 ________ if she finishes her homework in time.
5 ________ I'll see all my friends.
6 If I ________ , ________

3 In groups, share your sentences. Who wrote the most interesting sentence?

Mission Stage 1

Find out the class's technological need and choose your group's favourite!

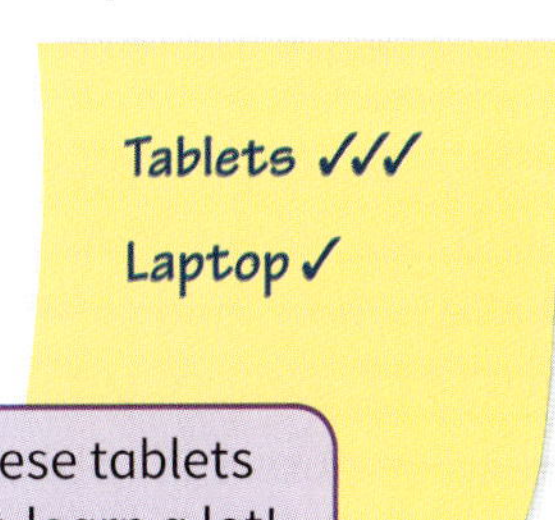

1 **Read the school webpage.** Who has a robot that gives food to cats? ______________

Wall | Find friends | Chat | Profile

JIM

Hi friends,

How will computers be different in 10 years' time? How will they help us? I'm making a poster about the future of computers and need ideas!

Thanks

Jim

In 10 years' time, I think there will be lots of computers in our homes. In fact, I think that we'll **chat** to computers all day.

The computers will help us a lot. If I'm hungry, I'll ask the freezer, 'What ice cream have we got?' Or if I take photos, I'll ask my phone to **upload** them to my blog. – Ibcat2

In 10 years' time, I think we'll stop using mice. Instead, we'll control our computers using our bodies. When we want to **click** on something, we'll close one eye. And, when we want to **download** a game or a film, we'll look down at the floor.

If we want to **turn on** a computer or **turn** it **off**, maybe we'll jump in the air! – CoolJen

If a computer has a small problem, like a broken 'enter' key, people often throw it away. But in the future computers will be easier to repair. Maybe we'll be able to **install** programs or borrow robots that repair our computers? And if our computers break, they'll be easy to recycle. – SofySky

My uncle's got lots of robots. If the floor is dirty, a robot drives around and cleans it. Another robot feeds his cats if they're hungry and **texts** his mobile phone when he needs to buy more cat food!

In 10 years' time, the computers in robots will be able to do almost anything. They'll help us by writing **emails** and doing our homework! – Jungles17

2 1.18 **Match the icons (1–9) to the words in bold on the webpage.** Then listen and check.

1 is 'chat'.

3 **Read the webpage again. Who says each sentence?**

1 'My friends and my sister are helping me with a project.'

I think Jim said this.

2 'Before I go outside, my cupboard will tell me if I need an umbrella.'

3 'Computers in the future will be easier to fix.'

4 'In the future, we'll be able to install programs by smiling.'

5 'In 10 years' time, a computer will be able to make Jim's poster for him.'

4 **Say sentences with the words from Activity 2.**

I chat with my friends online on Saturdays.

Grammar look: the zero and first conditional

'If the floor is dirty, a robot drives around and cleans.'

'If I'm hungry, I'll ask the freezer, "What ice cream have we got?"'

1 When the floor is dirty, how likely is it that the robot will clean? **Yes, the robot will clean. / Yes, the robot might clean.**

2 What kind of sentence is this? **Zero conditional / First conditional**

3 Will the boy be able to talk to the freezer in the future? **Yes, he will. / Yes, he might.**

4 What kind of sentence is this? **Zero conditional / First conditional**

5 We use the first conditional to talk about things that might happen. We use the zero conditional to talk about things that are **never / always** true.

page 120

1 What do you do now and what will you do in the future? Ask and answer.

1 Your computer doesn't turn on.
2 Your keyboard's 'enter' key is broken.
3 You want to chat to your friends.
4 You want to download a game.
5 Your floor is dirty.

At the moment, if my computer doesn't turn on, I ask my dad to help me.

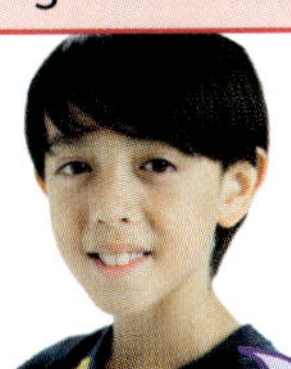

In the future, if my computer doesn't turn on, I'll be able to repair it on my own.

Mission Stage 2

Show how your piece of technology works.

If you install this program you can practise your English.

2 Write notes about how computers will be different in 10 years' time. How will they help us?

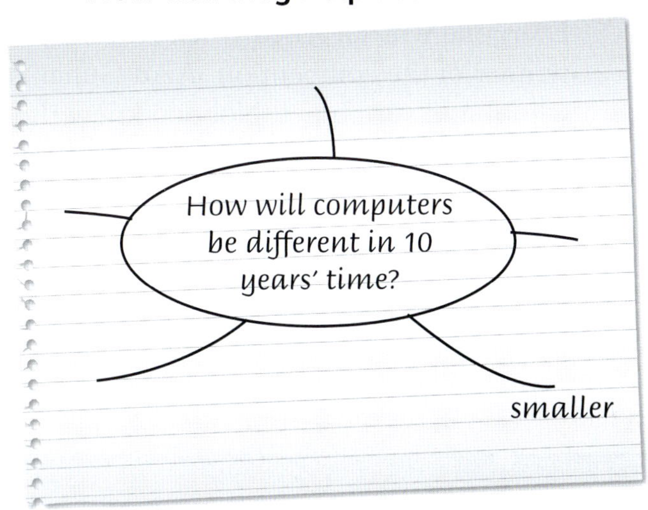

1 **What are the most popular newspapers in your country?** Does your school have its own newspaper or news section on its website?

1.19

THE IAST TIMES

If it happens, we write about it

Friday 28th May | iasttimes.co.tr | No 134

AZRA WINS!

The winner of The Istanbul Academy of Science and Technology's Design-an-app Competition surprised everyone. Emre Erdem tells us what happened.

This Monday there was a surprise winner of Dr Şafak's Design-an-app Competition. Azra Guner, who only joined the Academy last month, won first prize for her brilliant Timetabler app, which helps students organise their time.

Dr Şafak announced the competition at the beginning of May. She said, 'The app must be easy to install and use on a mobile phone, and it must help students with their schoolwork. It shouldn't use lots of battery.' Throughout the month this newspaper followed the competition. We spoke to students about possible winners and everyone said the same thing: 'If Burak Gül enters it, he'll win it.' 'Burak knows everything about computers,' said Ahmet Terim. 'His parents teach him.' 'He'll be the Steve Jobs of Turkey one day,' said Mira Balta.

Everyone was surprised when Dr Şafak announced the winner of the competition. Azra Guner is new to the school and very quiet. Nobody knew that she designed her first app when she was only seven years old. Now, she is the star of the software class and everyone wants to talk about her app. 'It makes it easy to plan your time!' said Hasan Can. 'I love it!' said Ecrin Bartu. 'With Azra's app, I can make a timetable really quickly!'

PROFILES

Name: Burak Gül
Age: 11
Interests: chess, reading

Name: Azra Guner
Age: 11
Interests: video games, music

Although Burak was very unhappy when he lost the competition, some students say that he and Azra are going to design a new app together. If that happens, you'll be able to read all about it in the *IAST Times*.

AN INTERVIEW WITH THE WINNER

What does your app do?

AZRA It makes a timetable for students.

Can you explain that?

AZRA Of course! You tell the app what exams you need to study for. You also tell it when the exams are. Then you click on the special 'plan' button and the app makes a timetable for you.

Do you mean it tells you what to study and when?

AZRA Yes, that's right! That means you have more time for studying because the app does the planning for you.

Technology Fact of the Week

Ada Lovelace was an English mathematician and one of the first computer programmers. In 1843 she wrote a program for a type of computer that was invented by an Englishman called Charles Babbage.

2 **In pairs, role play a conversation. Imagine you are Azra and Burak.**

STUDENT A You are Azra. You feel happy because you won the competition. You have lots of ideas for new apps. Ask Burak if he would like to help you design a new app.

I can't believe I won!

STUDENT B You are Burak. You feel jealous of Azra because you wanted to win the competition. Ask Azra about her app.

Cross-curricular

1 **Which apps do you use?** What do they do?

2 1.20 **Listen and read the text.** What do these numbers mean?

2 million $1 million 400 million

< What's an app? >

< There are lots of apps that you can download to a smartphone or laptop. The most popular are games, news, weather and social media apps. If you have an app on your phone, you just have to click on it. This means you don't need to search for a program or write the address of a website. One of the first apps was a game called 'Snake'. Players had to make a line of dots around the small screen. This might not sound very interesting, but 400 million people played this simple game. Now there are over 2 million apps to choose from. >

< How do you make an app? >

< Companies can spend between $50,000–$1 million on making apps. That's a lot of money! But if you have a good idea, you can make an app and create it for free. There are a few things to do if you want to make an app:

1 Think about what your app is going to do, how it will be good for the people using it and how you will let people know about your app. Write your ideas on a piece of paper and draw pictures.

2 Go online and check if there are other apps like yours. If there are, how is yours better?

3 Wireframe your idea. A wireframe is like a storyboard. You draw your design idea so that you can see what your app does. There are lots of different wireframing websites to help you do this.

4 Learn the language of app building. Lots of schools have coding clubs which teach you the languages you need to build apps. You need to choose a coding language and learn the rules. For example, when you are using HTML5, you need to use these symbols < > at the beginning and end of your codes. >

3 **In pairs, talk about about the sentences.** Say *yes* or *no* and why.

1 I'd like to play 'Snake'.
2 I'd like a maths app.
3 I think making an app is easy.
4 I'd like to make my own app.

A mobile phone is more powerful than the computer that sent astronauts to the moon in 1969.

1 Watch the video to see an example of Speaking Part 1.

2 Match the question words with the phrases. What information should the answer have?

What…?	A thing
Where…?	A time
Who…?	A place
When…?	A short description
Tell me about…	A person

3 Match the questions (1–6) to answers (A–F).

1 What's your family name?
2 Where are you from?
3 What do you like about your school?
4 Where did you go on holiday last year?
5 Who usually cooks in your house?
6 Tell me something about a new hobby you would like to try.

A I'm from Seville but I live in Madrid.
B It's Bowring.
C My family and I went to Corfu in Greece.
D It's got a big gym and a modern computer room.
E When I finish my exams, I'll start a short course on writing programs for computer games.
F My parents usually do the cooking but my brother is quite good at making curries and desserts!

4 In pairs, ask and answer the questions.

Hello, I'm Sally. Can I have your mark sheets please? Thank you.

What's your name?	I'm …
Do you like clothes shopping?	Yes, I go with … I like to buy …
Where do you go at the weekend?	I go to the …
What's your favourite subject at school?	I like … and … . Oh, and … of course!
When do you watch films?	On … I usually … with my friends.
Where do you usually have lunch?	Sometimes … but I often …
Tell me something about your family.	Well, I've got …

EXAM TIP! Try to **speak clearly** and remember to give **as much information** as you can!

1 Do the quick quiz.

1 What is a blog?

a a sauce b an animal
c something to read

2 Who can write a blog?

a anyone b children
c adults

3 Where can I read a blog?

a in a comic b online
c in a book

2 In the exam you read about three people talking about the same thing. You have to decide which person says something. What do you think is the best way to do this? Choose and put the sentences in order.

A read each text once
B read the questions
C choose a letter
D read the three texts again

______ ______
______ ______

3 Choose the correct answer.

1 Which person doesn't write as much as before?

a Now I'm nineteen and I don't write my blog very often.

b I post a message once a week.

2 Which person sometimes gets a message they don't want?

a … sometimes I get emails from my school.

b Sometimes I get a strange message on the screen but I don't mind … I just delete it immediately!

3 Which person was the youngest when they started their blog?

a I started my blog when I was thirteen.

b I started blogging when I was twelve.

4 Which person needs some help to write their blog?

a My computer is so slow! Sometimes I need to ask if I can use my brother's.

b When the wifi is broken I can't post a new blog.

EXAM TIP! Don't worry if you see some words which you don't know. You will still be able to answer the question.

1 Match the sentence halves.

1 If the laptops are cheap, …
2 If I can't go to the park, …
3 If I want to do my homework on a computer, …
4 If you press 'enter', …
5 If her keyboard is broken, …

A the program will download.
B I'll chat to my friends online.
C I'll buy a new one today.
D Grandma won't be able to email me.
E I'll need a printer.

2 **Read the email.** Choose the correct answer.

Hi Jim,

Sorry for replying so slowly!

At the moment, when you order pizzas, they often **(1)** _____ slowly. When there **(2)** _____ a lot of traffic, the pizza can get cold too! In the future, I think that flying robots will carry pizzas. So **(3)** _____ you want one, it will be at your house in less than five minutes. **(4)** _____ you want the pizza cut up, the robot **(5)** _____ do that for you too!

– Mike

1	A arrive	B arrive	C arriving
2	A was	B will	C is
3	A while	B because	C if
4	A When	B Can	C Are
5	A able	B will	C is

EXAM TIP! Read the text **once** to understand it. Then read the text **again** and choose the best word for each space.

3 **Look at the new words from this unit.** Make puzzles with the words using the steps below.

Make a 'Find the different word' puzzle

- **Four kinds of hardware + one other word**
- **Four verbs + one other word**

Make one more puzzle.

- **Your own idea**
- **Four things you use with your hands + one other word**

Use it

Challenge a friend to find the different words in each of your puzzles.

Mission in action!

- **Present your group's ideas.**
- **Choose the best new technology for the class.**

3 Jim-nastics

1

2

3

4

5

6

7

8

9

What sports can you see in the pictures? Which of the sports is your favourite?

Watch the video. What goes wrong when Jim and Jenny play cricket?

Mission Invent a new sport

1. Make a mind map to compare sports.
2. Invent and describe a new sport.
3. ★ Play the sport and vote for the best one!

1 1.21 **Read the TV guide.** Match the words in blue to the pictures below. Then listen and check.

Rugby is number 7.

Wednesday, 9 October

	7:00	7:30	8:00	8:30
Sport 1	Rugby tonight: Wales vs. Australia		Deep diving: Daniel swims with sharks	
Sport 2	Small white ball: Exciting golf from around the world		Cricket chat: A review of today's cricket matches	
US Adventure	Cycling: A woman, her bike and America's biggest mountains	Ice-hockey special: See the skaters on the ice for Russia vs. Canada		Surfing: Hawaii's best surfers surf the ocean's biggest waves
FIT1	Be fit boxing: Get your gloves on and get fit	Gymnastics at home: Jump, dance and stretch with Paul	Be fit boxing: Get your gloves on and get fit	Gymnastics at home: Jump, dance and stretch with Paul
AllStars	Sports stars of tomorrow: Watch athletics stars run, throw and jump to prepare for the Olympics		Snow idea: Snow skiers try water-skiing for the first time on Lake Tahoe	

2 **Write the sports.**

Sports I've tried: ____________________

Sports I've not tried but would like to try: ____________________

Sports I just want to watch on TV: ____________________

3 ☆ **Do you like the sports in Activity 1? In pairs, say why or why not.**

I love cycling. I go every week with my dad and my brother. It's a great way to see the countryside. Do you like cycling?

EXAM TIP! Be ready to help your partner by repeating what you say or asking them questions.

For example:

Why don't you like …?

What do you think about …?

How about …?

1 **Read Jim's blog.** How many dogs can stand on a surfboard?

Jim's Big Blog

If you think that sports like golf or gymnastics aren't interesting enough, you might want to try something a little stranger. I've found three really unusual sports to tell you about.

The world's three strangest sports

The Mud Olympics

The Mud Olympics is held every year in a small German town called Brunsbuettel. Around 50 teams from different countries meet and play football and other sports in deep mud. As you can see, the players get very dirty! Yuck! There are lots of prizes – and people love playing in the mud – but the main reason that the event is arranged is to get money to give to charities.

Man versus Horse

This athletics event is held in Llanwrtyd Wells in Wales. At the event, men and women race a horse for 35 kilometres. People often think that the horse will win easily – but the race is planned so that the horse and runners finish at nearly the same time. How's that done? Well, there are lots of mountains near Llanwrtyd Wells and horses are very slow at going down hills!

Dog surfing

In this sport, the dog usually surfs with a person, but sometimes the dog surfs alone or two dogs surf on one board. Dog surfing competitions are organised by people all around the world. At one competition in the USA, someone took a photo of 18 dogs on a surfboard. That's the largest number ever! I wish I took that photo!

2 ☆ **Read the sentences and choose the correct event.**

	The Mud Olympics	Man vs. Horse	Dog Surfing
1 Pets do this event on their own, in pairs, or with a man or woman.	A	B	C
2 Groups do the event together.	A	B	C
3 The event happens in an area where there are lots of hills.	A	B	C
4 People collect money at the event.	A	B	C
5 Competitions happen in many different places.	A	B	C
6 The person or animal who finishes this event first is the winner.	A	B	C

EXAM TIP! Focus on the **general meaning** of the text and don't worry if there are some words that you don't know.

Grammar look: the passive (present simple)

'The race is planned so that the horse and runners finish at nearly the same time.'

'Dog surfing competitions are organised by people all around the world.'

1 Who plans the races in Man vs. Horse?
We don't know / The runners

2 Who organises dog surfing competitions?
We don't know / people all around the world

3 Which word says who organised the dog surfing competitions? **the / by**

We use the passive when we (4) **know / don't know** who does something or when it (5) **is / isn't** important who does something.

page 121

1 Complete the sentences. Use the words in brackets and the passive in the present simple.

How to plan a dog surfing competition

Ideas for the dog surfing event (1) are discussed (discuss). Plans (2) __________ (made) to be sure that the event is safe.

The dog surfers meet and the event starts. The winner of each competition (3) __________ (give) a prize – it could be a golden dog toy!

Photographs of the event (4) __________ (take) and (5) __________ (share) on the Internet.

Dog food, balls and other litter (6) __________ (clean) from the beach and everyone goes home.

Mission Stage 1

Make a mind map to compare your feelings about different sports.

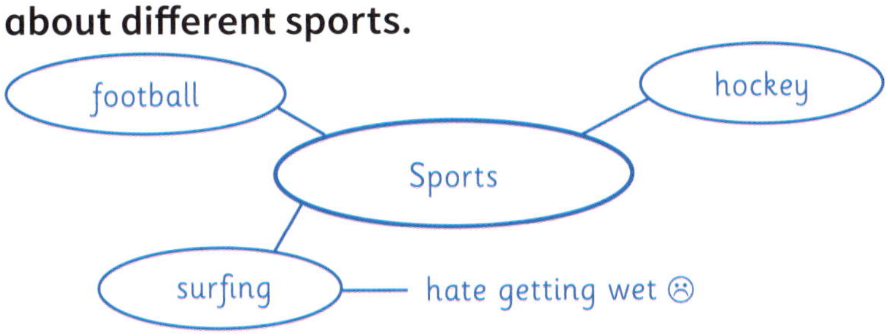

2 In pairs, say sentences and say which sport it is.

It's held every year.

The Mud Olympics.

Yes!

1 1.22 **Listen. Match the sports commentaries (1–4) to the photos (A–D).**

A ☐

B ☐

C ☐

D ☐

2 1.23 **Match the definitions (A–K) to the words (1–11). Listen and check.**

1 ☐ goal
2 ☐ coach
3 ☐ train
4 ☐ surfboard
5 ☐ net
6 ☐ hit
7 ☐ racket
8 ☐ court
9 ☐ cyclist
10 ☐ track
11 ☐ helmet

1 is J.

A to practise a sport, often to prepare for a competition

B to touch something quickly and hard

C the place where you play sports like tennis

D you wear this to keep your head safe

E a person who cycles

F the thing people stand on when they surf
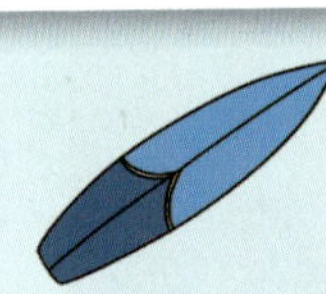

G something used to hit the ball in sports like tennis

H the thing in the middle of a tennis court that people hit the ball over
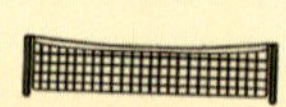

I a path used for races

J a point scored in a game like football
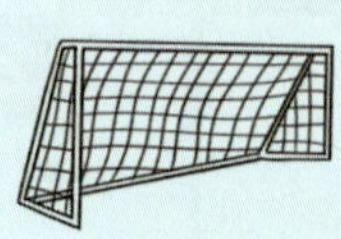

K someone who prepares a team to play sport

3 1.24 **Listen again.** Why are the numbers below important?

three minutes | 2–1 | 35 minutes | $1 million | one point | two metres | ten | eight

Grammar look: modal verbs

'Birch may have made a mistake.'

'This could be the most important point today.'

'The Silver Beach surfing competition will start in about 35 minutes.'

'Hugh hits it back well but the ball might go into the net!'

'Can Waldek shoot?'

'Shall we watch that goal again?'

1 Modal verbs **are** / **aren't** followed by the infinitive form of a verb without 'to' (e.g. *speak*, *go*, *walk* etc.)
2 When you use *he* or *she*, you **do** / **don't** need to add an 's' to the modal verb.
3 To make a question, you **do** / **don't** change the order of the modal (e.g. *might*, *will*, *can* etc.) and the subject (e.g. *I*, *you*, *he*, *she* etc.).
4 There **are** / **aren't** *-ing* forms of modal verbs.

page 121

1 1.25 **PRONUNCIATION Listen and repeat.** page 118

2 Read the dialogue and choose the correct words.

60%

Harley
online

(1) **Shall we** / **We shall** <u>play tennis</u> tonight?

Yes, (2) **would I** / **I'd like to**. But <u>it's cloudy outside. It may rain</u>.

If it rains, we (3) **can** / **might** <u>play table-tennis inside</u>.

Great!

Could you (4) **to bring** / **bring** <u>balls</u>, please?

I don't have any. But I can ask my brother. He (5) **might** / **shall** be able to <u>lend us some</u>.

OK. I'll see you later then.

See you later!

3 Act out the dialogue. Then act it out again, changing the underlined words.

4 Choose a sport and write a short sports commentary. How many modal verbs can you use?

We're here at the lake to watch the water-skiing today, and we might be lucky with the weather ...

Mission Stage 2

Invent and describe a new sport.

1 **Look at the pictures.** What kind of text is it? Do you like these kinds of stories?

1.27

The Spartan Princess

In Ancient Greece, around 428 BCE …

Cynisca is a young Greek princess. She is a Spartan. It's hard being a Spartan. They are only interested in being very fit. Boys practise fighting and do athletics and girls also do a lot of exercise. It isn't different for Cynisca even though she's a princess. Her dad, Archidamus, King of Sparta, has encouraged her to do all kinds of sports since she was very young, such as riding and running just like her brother Agesilaus. Cynisca's favourite sport is chariot racing.

When the king dies, Cynisca receives half of his money. Agesilaus gets the other half and becomes King. Cynisca really wants to compete in the Olympics so she decides to buy the horses and the chariot she needs.

Cynisca trains the horses for the chariot races every day for a year.

3

Cynisca finally finds a charioteer. He's perfect for the job. He's thin, tall and young. She is a strong instructor.

The summer of 396 BCE …

Finally, the day of the Olympic Games arrives. Cynisca travels with her brother and horses to the great stadium of Zeus at Olympia. The games are held here every four years. The streets are crowded. People come to watch and take part in the games from all over the world, from as far away as Spain and Turkey.

Cynisca sits outside the stadium and listens to the crowds shouting and screaming. The four-horse chariot race is always the most spectacular race in the Olympics.

My family and I were Kings and Queens. I, Cynisca who won with a four-horse chariot, put up this statue. I am the only woman in Greece to win this prize.

Cynisca wasn't able to take part herself in the Olympic Games, but she won the chariot race twice in 396 BCE and again in 392 BCE.

2 In pairs, talk about the questions.

1. How do you think Cynisca felt about not riding the chariot herself in the games?
2. What kind of person was Cynisca? How did this help her enter and win the Olympic Games twice?
3. What was Cynisca's relationship with her brother?
4. Why do you think there is a statue to remember Cynisca?

1 **Look at the pictures.** How do these activities help you to prepare for a sports competition?

2 1.28 **Listen and read the text.** How many hours a day does each athlete train?

Every four years the Olympics is shown on TV. It takes years of training and hard work to compete at an Olympic Games and there are many things that an athlete has to think about before they run around the track, hit a ball or put on a helmet for that important race.

Gymnasts

Training: Gymnasts train for six hours a day. As well as this, they swim, cycle and run to make their legs stronger. It's important that they stretch every part of their body before and after they practise or they might get injured.

Food: Gymnasts need to eat a lot of protein (chicken and fish) and healthy snacks like bananas and strawberries.

Rest: They have one rest day a week and try to get a good night's sleep too. It's difficult to train if you are tired.

Simone Biles has got the most medals of any American gymnast.

Divers

Training: Divers also train for about six hours a day, but before they get into the pool, they have to practise in the gym. They lift weights and do handstands to make their forearms strong. After training in the pool they often put ice on their triceps to help them recover.

Food: Food is very important for divers. Cereal with lots of iron in is good and it's important in the evening to eat snacks with carbohydrates like toast with chocolate spread – this helps with energy levels.

Rest: After training all day, divers often have a massage and they are in bed by 10:30 pm.

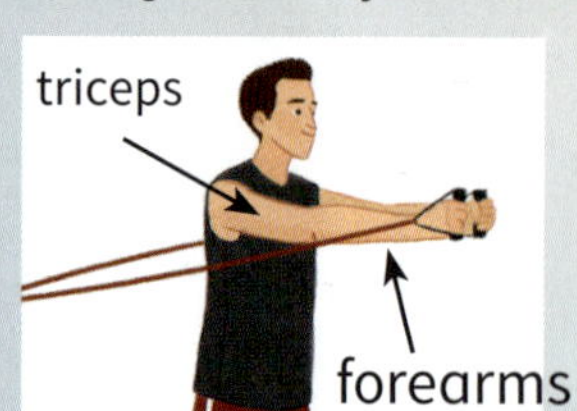

Tom Daley is the youngest ever British World Champion in any sport.

3 **Read the text again and answer the questions.**

1 How often can you watch the Olympic Games?

2 What do athletes need to do before competing?

3 Why should athletes stretch before and after training?

4 Why shouldn't athletes go to bed late?

5 How do athletes look after their muscles?

6 Write examples of each of the food groups:
Protein: … Iron: … Carbohydrates: …

1 1.29 **Look at the example answer and listen.** What will the children learn?

Surf Camp

When: Summer

2 1.30 **Match the correct type of information (1–7) to the words in bold.** There are two extra answers. Listen and check.

1 A food
2 A place
3 An age
4 A price
5 A time
6 A name
7 A body part

A Surfing might look hard and your **stomach** might hurt …
B Your gym coach is Bob Vanya, that's **V-A-N-Y-A**.
C Half of your food needs to be water, **fruit** and vegetables …
D We think **45** minutes a day is enough!
E If you want help choosing your meals, I'll be in the Main **Hall** …

3 1.31 **Listen again and write the correct answer in the gap.** Use the words in bold from Activity 2.

Camp

When:	Summer
Food:	(6) 50% water, ________ and vegetables 50% meat and sugars
Help with meals:	(7) Main ________ after 6 pm
Use Gym:	(8) After every lesson for ________ minutes
Name of coach:	(9) Bob ________
First day:	(10) ________ might hurt.

EXAM TIP! The answer could be a **word** or a **number**. You may also need to **spell a name**.

1 Read the text and answer the questions.

1 Who is Billy? Billy is Henry's friend.
2 Where is he?
3 What sport is he doing?
4 Who is he writing to?

From: Billy **To:** Henry

Hi Henry,

How (1) are you? I'm trying a new sport called cricket. It's not like baseball but it's very popular here (2) in India! I've got (3) a great coach. He's called Kishan and before he became a coach he played in a famous (4) team.

Yesterday our group practised in the park. Kishan showed (5) us how to hold the bat and hit the ball. Later, Mum and I watched a match. Kishan (6) was playing with his new team and they won! Afterwards Kishan said I could keep the ball!

I'll send you (7) some photos after my lesson.

Write to me soon!

Billy

2 Look at the underlined words in Activity 1. What type of words are they?

- verb
- indefinite article
- preposition
- pronoun
- auxiliary verb
- noun

3 Complete the email. Use the words in the box.

went I my the for

From: Henry **To:** Billy

Dear Billy,

Thanks (1) ________ your message. Cricket sounds like a lot of fun.

I'm on holiday with (2) ________ family in Sri Lanka, which is near India. We (3) ________ cycling this morning and then I took my surfboard to (4) ________ beach in the afternoon.

Talk soon!

Henry

1 Rewrite the sentences in the passive. Don't use the underlined word.

1 People hold The Mud Olympics every year.
The Mud Olympics is held every year.

2 People play lots of different sports.

3 People play football.

4 People sell tickets to raise money for charity.

5 Someone gives prizes to the winners of the competition.

6 People need lots of showers at the event.

2 Write the sentences in the negative and question form.

1 You can play cricket well.
You can't play cricket well.
Can you play cricket well?

2 I could hit the ball.

3 You should train every day.

4 We can go water-skiing here.

5 I may get a surfboard from that shop.

6 I will play ice hockey.

3 Choose ten words from this unit. Record the words using the steps below.

Find the meaning
→ In this unit / In a dictionary

Record its meaning
→ Write the word in your language / Write the definition

Use it
→ Say the meaning of the word to a partner. Can they guess it?

Mission in action!

- Present the new sport.
- Play the sport and give tips.
- Vote for the best!

How to win at my sport:

- Don't forget a helmet! Then you won't be scared.
- You don't need to worry about the other players.

Review ••• Units 1–3

1 Watch the video and do the quiz.

2 Complete the text. Use the words in the box.

dull as as boring as interesting as exciting as
as strong and thin big and strong as

Some people say that athletics isn't (1) ________ other sports. They say that watching people run is (2) ________ as watching paint dry. But I don't agree! The ends of athletics races are as (3) ________ when someone scores a goal in a sport like football or ice hockey. And, when you watch athletics you see lots of different events. Some athletes have to be as (4) ________ rugby players or boxers. Other athletes have to be (5) ________ as gymnasts. I think the most boring sport is cricket. I don't like golf either – I think that's nearly as (6) ________ cricket.

3 Complete the sentences. Use the words in brackets and the present simple with future meaning.

(1) ________ *(The water skiing instructor / finish) work on 15 July. Ask at reception if you'd like to write a message in her card.*

Hi everyone – please arrive by 8 am for tomorrow's ***Runners vs. Cyclists race.***

(2) ________ (Cyclists / start) at 8:45.
(3) ________ (Runners / start) at 8 am.

Do you need surfboards or a swimming costume?

(4) ________ (Our new surfboard shop / open) next Monday at 9:00 am. Come and see us at 15 Beach Road.

Would you like to join our new rugby team?
(5) ________ (we have) our first training session after school on Friday and we play weekly. Call Francesca on 07700 900245 for more information.

BALANCE
fitness for everyone

4 Complete the text.

(1) If it's sunny at the weekend, I (2) ________ go shopping with my friend, Sue. We'll go to the town centre and look in the shops. There are holes in my jumper's sleeves, so (3) ________ there's a sale, I'll buy a new one. (4) ________ get one with a cool pattern, (5) ________ I can find a pattern I like. Sue wants to buy a leather handbag – I think (6) ________ buy one if it's not too expensive.

5 What are you going to do this weekend? Who will you spend time with? Write 25–35 words.

6 Say six sentences.

If	+	you like the tracksuit you get brown leather shoes it snows later my blouses are dirty my swimming costume is wet the jewellery isn't expensive	+	my mum will wear her raincoat. they'll look good with your brown trousers. I'll get a new gold chain. I borrow clean ones from my sister. you should try it on. I put it in the garden to dry.

7 Find the mistakes. Write the correct sentences.

1 My best friend it is called Luisa. ______

2 In my bedroom there's a bed which made of wood.

______

3 My favourite song is call **One Last Time**.

______

The school discos are organised the teachers.

5 The food is choose by my cousin.

______

6 They eat special cakes which make for the wedding.

______

8 Choose the correct words to complete the sentences.

1 I **wouldn't** / **might not** like to chat to my favourite singer. I'm too shy.

2 Can you **download** / **downloading** these pictures for me, please?

3 Could you **texting** / **text** Grandma and ask her what time she's coming?

4 He **shall** / **might** email me after dinner.

5 **I may** / **May I** turn on the TV, please?

6 **Shall I install** / **Install I shall** this software for you?

9 Choose and complete two of the challenges.

CHALLENGE 1

Look at Unit 1. Find three:

- things people wear when they exercise.
- parts of a shirt.
- things people wear over shirts.
- things clothes are made of.

CHALLENGE 2

Look at Unit 2 pages 17 and 20. What are five things your computer has got? What are five things your computer can do?

CHALLENGE 3

Find a sports word in Unit 3 that starts with each of the following letters:

B-I-R-D-W-A-T-C-H-E-R-S

4 Be careful!

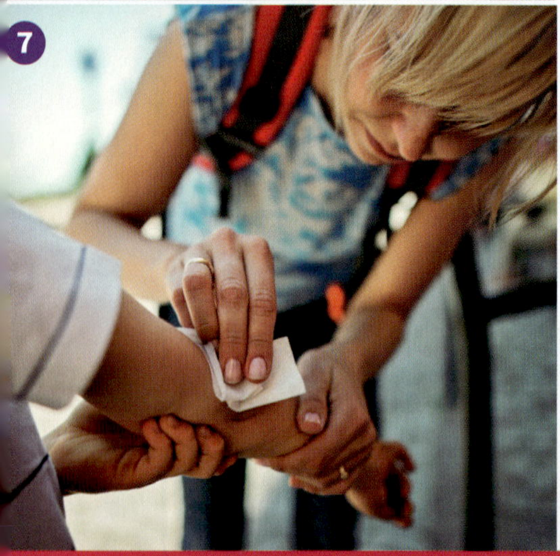

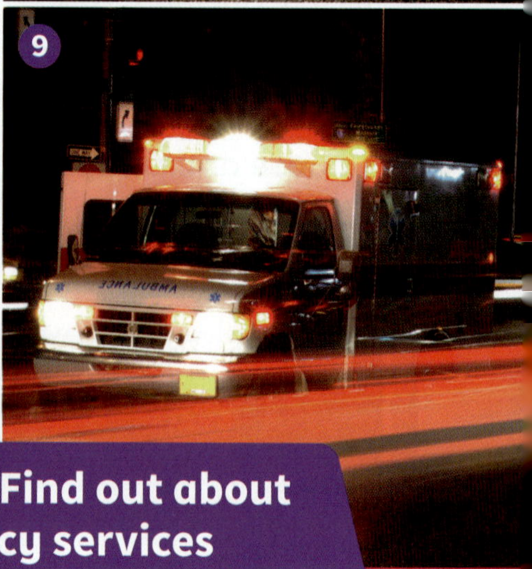

What ways of staying safe can you see in the pictures?

Watch the video. Which was the best way of making Jim feel better?

Mission Find out about emergency services

1. Make a list of questions about the emergency services.
2. Find answers to your questions about the emergency services.
3. ★ Present what you have found out.

1 2.02 **Listen and choose the correct answer.**

1 The shark bit the man when he was …

A looking for a golf ball. B swimming. C feeding his pet.

2 The fire started because of …

A the monster. B someone cooking. C a candle falling.

3 The man with the big hands hurt himself when he was …

A using scissors. B preparing food. C playing in the park.

EXAM TIP! Read the questions **before** the listening starts.

2 2.03 **Complete the sentences. Use the words in the box. Then listen and check.**

injured	break	appointment	cut	painful	heart	accident	ankle	emergency door	patient

1 Yes, he __________ his hand when he was feeding his shark.

2 I've made an __________ for the man to meet the doctor.

3 What's wrong with this __________ ? The man who's having his __________ checked.

4 That woman's running to the __________ . Do you know why there's a fire?

5 I think there was an __________ and her pet monster made the fire.

6 Did the monster __________ the woman's __________ , too?

7 While he was making a sandwich, his knife slipped and he __________ his hand.

8 It looks very __________ . It must hurt a lot.

3 **In pairs, ask and answer about the picture in Activity 2.**

What's wrong with this man?

He's injured his hand.

1 VIKTOR, JIM FRIENDLIE

Hi Jim – how are you? 8:27

I haven't been well for a week. 8:27

Jenny told me. Did you get our card? 8:28

Yes – thank you! 8:29

I want to come back soon though to see you all. But I feel awful! 8:29

Yeah, but you need to stay in bed if you want to get better. Drink lots of water! 8:30

I will. 8:31

Can't wait to see you again. 8:31

You too. 8:32

2 ELIZABETH, ALEX

Hi Alex– would you like to come to the park later? 7:04

No, sorry. I need to take my rabbit to the vet. 7:07

Oh no! What's wrong with her? 7:08

She's had a problem with her heart since April. 7:09

7:10

Poor thing! I hope she's better soon. 7:10

Me too! The vet says that she'll be fine. 7:11

3 JULIA, IAN

I've broken my ankle . 4:21

I was playing tennis in the courts in the park when a dog ran towards me. I tried to get away by jumping over the net but I fell over it and broke my ankle . 4:21

Oh no! How long has your ankle been injured? 4:22

Since Tuesday. I've been at home since then. 4:22

Is it painful? 4:22

No, it's fine – but I feel very bored. I haven't left my house for days!

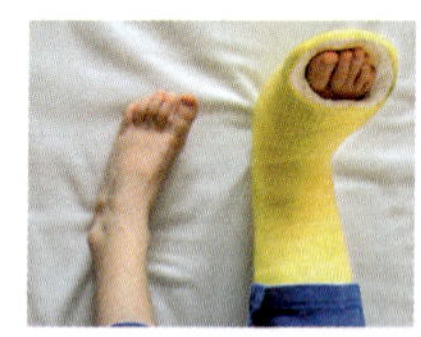

4:23

What have you studied in chemistry since Tuesday? I'd like to look at it this week. 4:24

Pages 46 and 47. 4:27

Shall I visit this evening? We could look at the chemistry together. 4:27

Thank you! That'd be great. 4:28

I'll bring you some chocolates to help you feel better . 4:29

1 ★ **Look at the messages again. Choose the correct answer.**

1 Why is Viktor writing to Jim?

A He's worried about his friend. B He's going to get Jim a glass of water. C He wants Jim to write a card.

2 Why did Elizabeth write to Alex?

A Her rabbit is unwell. B She's going to go to the vet with him. C She wanted to go to the park with him.

3 What do Julia and Ian agree to do together?

A eat sweets B study chemistry C walk the dog

EXAM TIP! After you've chosen A, B or C, read the text and the question again to **check** that **your answer** is correct.

Grammar look: the present perfect with *how long*, *for* and *since*

'I haven't been well for a week.'
'She's had a problem with her heart since April.'

1 When did Jim start feeling unwell? **a week ago** / **Monday**

2 Does the rabbit still have a problem? **Yes** / **No**

We use the present perfect to describe actions that started in the (3) **past** / **present** and are still happening in the (4) **present** / **future**.

With (5) ***I, you, they* and *we*** / ***he, she* and *it*** we use *have* + past participle (e.g. *made, done, eaten* etc.)

With (6) ***I, you, they* and *we*** / ***he, she* and *it*** we use *has* + past participle.

page 122

1 2.04 **PRONUNCIATION Listen and repeat.** page 118

2 Write six true sentences. Use the phrases in the box or your own ideas.

I haven't had a cold I've lived in my house I haven't felt sick I've been at this school I've studied geography I haven't eaten chocolate	for	a few hours. three weeks. a month. five years. a long time. as long as I can remember.
	since	Monday. this morning. 23rd January. yesterday. last winter. I was born.

____

____

____

____

____

____

3 In pairs, share your sentences from Activity 2. Who hasn't felt sick for the longest time?

Mission Stage 1

Make a list of questions about the emergency services.

How can I call the emergency services?

Who will come?

What sound does an ambulance make?

Did you know?

A long time ago, when people had sore throats, they tried to get better by putting dirty socks around their necks. Some people put fish on their feet too!

1 **Read the diary.** What happened to Dizzy at the lake?

4th August

I'm excited because tomorrow I'm going to the hills with my aunt. I'm going to take my dog, Dizzy for a walk and then we're going to go swimming in a lake. We're not going home until after dinner!

My aunt's meeting us tomorrow at 9 am to drive us there – so I should go to sleep now. ☺

5th August

Today something awful happened. We were having a lovely day in the hills – Dizzy was happy and we had a lovely picnic. But when we went to the lake, things started to go wrong.

We were swimming when Dizzy cut her leg badly on a rock. She fell over and started crying. We put a **bandage** round her leg and carried her back to the car.

It looks really painful so we're taking her to the vet this evening. ☹

6th August

The vet gave Dizzy a **prescription** for some **pills**, and she said that Dizzy needs to have a small **operation**.

Also, I think I've got the **flu**. When I got out of the lake, I was so worried about Dizzy that I forgot to get warm and dry. My mum's given me some medicine for my headache. She told me to go to bed and rest. But when I **lie down**, I can't sleep because I'm so worried about Dizzy.

7th August

I've got some great news. Dizzy's operation was a success! Dizzy's **resting** at the vet's at the moment and the vet says she can come home tomorrow. Hooray!

I'm **feeling better** too. So I'll be able to look after Dizzy when she gets home.

2 **Match the words in bold in the diary to the pictures below.**

Number 1 is 'resting'.

1 
2 
3 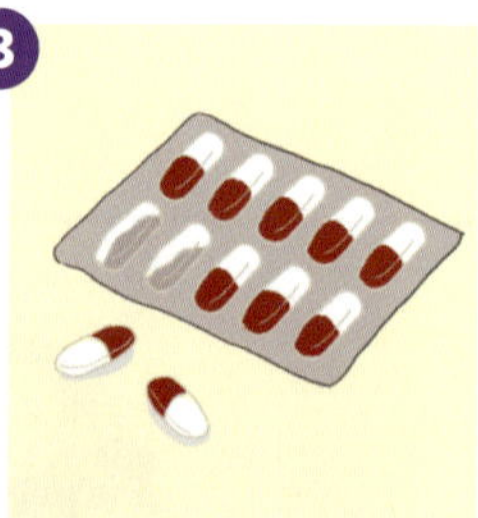
4 
5 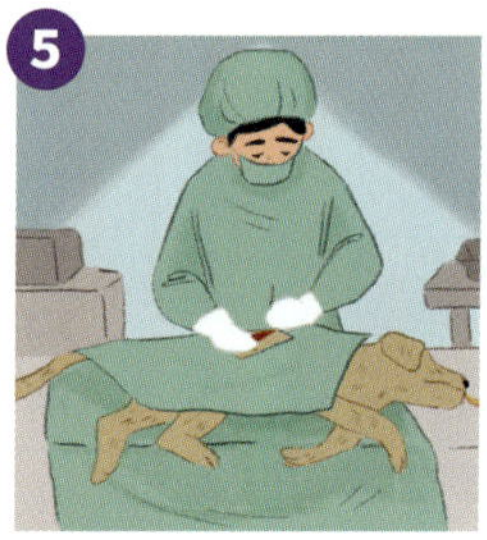
6 
7 
8 

3 **Add one sentence (A–D) to the end of each day's diary entry.**

A I wonder what she'll say.
B I can't wait to see her again!
C I hope her operation is OK.
D I'm so excited about the trip.

Grammar look: the present continuous for future plans

'We're taking her to the vet this evening.'
'We're not going home until after dinner!'

1 When will Dizzy go to the vet? **In the future** / **now**
2 Will Dizzy definitely go to the vet? **Yes** (they've made the plan) / **No** (they'll make the plan this evening)

1 The present continuous can be used to talk about the present and the **past** / **future**.
2 The present continuous is used to talk about the future when something is **uncertain** / **planned** and we say when it will happen.

page 122

1 **Look at Jenny's calendar.** Complete the sentences below using the present continuous.

My plans!

	Monday	Tuesday	Wednesday	Thursday	Friday	Saturday	Sunday
today	17 6 pm – make cookies for my family	18 lunchtime – go to athletics club	19 	20 after school – get Jim a present (not flowers!)	21 evening – do my maths homework	22 film the video diary	23 

1 At 6 pm today, Jenny's making ___________
2 ___________ at lunchtime tomorrow.
3 ___________ on Thursday after school.
4 On Friday evening, ___________

At 6 pm today, Jenny's making cookies for her family.

5 At the weekend, ___________
6 On Wednesday, ___________

2 **In pairs, talk about your plans.** How many are the same?

What are you doing …

… at 6 pm today?
… tomorrow lunchtime?
… on Thursday after school?
… on Friday evening?
… at the weekend?

What are you doing after school today?

I'm going to watch an ice-hockey match!

Mission Stage 2

Find answers to your questions about the emergency services.

Search Emergency services contact
About 9,397 results (0.21 seconds)
In England, the number you need to call for an ambulance is 999.

1 **Read the title of the story.** What do you think it's going to be about?

2.06

The £20,000 adventure

Joshua's ill and bored. He has flu, and he has had a fever for several days. But today he's feeling a bit better. His mum says he can go downstairs, lie down on the sofa and watch television with his sister, Chloe.

Joshua and Chloe are watching a programme about crocodiles. There's a knock on the door. It's their cousin, Eddie. He has come to see if Joshua's feeling better. 'How long have you been ill?' he asks. 'For four days,' says Joshua. 'I haven't been to school since last Monday!' 'Lucky you!' says Eddie.

The crocodile programme has finished. The local news programme is starting. 'There was a robbery at Whitton's bank last night. Unfotunately, thieves stole about £20,000 in cash and escaped in a fast car,' the newsreader says. 'The thieves are dangerous criminals.'

'I know that bank,' Chloe says excitedly. 'It's on the High Street.' Joshua's feeling sleepy. His eyes are closing! 'Come on, Joshua,' says Eddie. 'Let's climb some trees.'

★ ★ ★

Outside in the garden Chloe's climbing a tree and the two boys quickly climb up to join her. 'Look at those men!' says Chloe, pointing at two men kneeling on the ground by the river. 'What are they doing?' 'Shhhhhh!' whispers Joshua. 'They'll hear you and they look dangerous!' 'But look!' says Eddie, feeling worried. 'What *are* they doing?'

One of the men is taking a huge pile of papers from a brown bag. 'It's the £20,000!' whispers Chloe. 'You know – the money from the bank on the High Street. Look! They're hiding it in the hole.' 'Yes, and the newsreader said they're dangerous criminals,' whispers Joshua.

The two men look up as if they've heard something. The children freeze – they are terrified.

The three children watch in complete silence while the men finish hiding the cash and walk away through the wood. 'Let's get it!' says Chloe, climbing down the tree fast. 'Come on, Joshua,' shouts Eddie. 'What are you waiting for? They might come back.' But Joshua isn't feeling well. He thinks he might have a fever again. As he's climbing down the tree he cuts his knee and cries out in pain.

Chloe and Eddie get the bag. They make so much noise that Joshua starts to feel nervous. They don't see the men coming back! Suddenly, the men are standing right behind them and they look furious. 'Hey! Drop that!' they shout. 'Run!' shouts Eddie.

Eddie and Chloe grab the money and run to the bridge as fast as they can. They cross over the river. But Joshua can't run to the bridge. His knee's bleeding. It's too painful to run. 'Hurry up, Joshua, they're going to catch you,' shouts Eddie from the other side of the river.

Joshua decides to swim to the other side. He's just going to jump into the water to cross the river, when he sees crocodiles. He's very frightened now.

'Oh no, crocodiles – how strange!' thinks Joshua for a moment. 'Crocodiles live in Africa, not here!'

Joshua's trapped with the thieves behind him and crocodiles in front of him! Oh no! He can't run to the bridge. He can't swim across the river. What can he do? Then he sees a rope hanging from a tree. Can he swing across?

★ ★ ★

'Joshua, wake up! You're shouting in your sleep … something about crocodiles. Are you feeling OK?' asks his mother, coming into the room.

'Oh, Mum. Yes, I'm feeling much better now!' says Joshua.

'Come on. Switch off the television. It's time to eat,' says his mum.

2 In pairs, talk about the questions.

1 Which real-life facts were in Joshua's dream?
2 What do you think of Chloe and Eddie's actions in the story? What would you have done?
3 How do you think Joshua feels when he sees the crocodiles? What does he do to help himself?

1 **Look at the pictures.** What do you think they show?

2 2.07 **Listen and read the text.** Check your answers to Activity 1.

What was life like in the 1700s?

Many poor people didn't eat very well and so when they were ill, they could die. Lots of families had one toilet in the garden and it wasn't very clean. They also didn't have soap (and sometimes no water) to wash their hands. Doctors didn't know very much about what different illnesses were and they didn't have medicines to give people. Children also didn't have vaccinations to prevent them from getting ill and so they got illnesses like measles, chicken pox and flu.

How is life different now?

Doctors have learned a lot about preventing illnesses since the 1940s. We are told to eat a balanced diet and we also know that it's important to wash our hands before we eat or if you cut yourself. Before the 1940s if you cut your finger, bacteria could get into the cut and so lots of people died from a disease called tetanus. Now, we have vaccinations at the doctor. This is an injection to stop us getting the disease. Vaccinations contain a small amount of a virus or bacteria that help the body to fight the disease.

Sir Alexander Fleming (1881–1955): In 1928, Sir Alexander Fleming discovered penicillin and this helped to develop a group of medicines called antibiotics.

During World War I he saw lots of soldiers die from infected cuts.

He started growing germs in dishes to study them.

In 1928 he noticed mould was growing in his dishes and killing the germs.

This was penicillin and it has saved the lives of millions of people.

3 **Read the text again and say *yes* or *no*.**

1. Some people didn't have water in the past.
2. Children had injections to stop them getting ill in the past.
3. In 1928 you could die if you cut your finger.
4. A vaccination gives you a disease.
5. Alexander Fleming died in World War I.
6. He wasn't trying to grow mould.

4 **In pairs, talk about the best treatment for the problems in the box.**

a nosebleed   a cold   a headache   a cut knee

1 Read the words. What are the differences in meaning?

study / studio / studied doctor / medicine / bandage who / when / where

and / but / because century / years / months open / opened / opening

2 Which words in Activity 1 do you use to talk about …

- a period of 100 years?
- a question word about a person?
- a person who tells you what medicine to take when you are ill?

3 Complete the sentences with the words from Activity 1.

1 Why did Jim cut his arm? __________ he fell off his bike yesterday.

2 __________ was Fred having a rest? In his bedroom.

3 Last week we __________ the heart and brain in biology.

4 Her coach put a __________ around her leg and then she felt better.

5 Julie started rugby lessons in February and she broke her finger two __________ later in April.

6 I'd like to __________ a hospital for sick animals.

4 Read the text. What is it about?

Elizabeth Blackwell

Elizabeth was born in the south-west of England but in 1831 she moved to New York with her family. She started to work as a teacher there. She really wanted to **(1)** ______ medicine so she found some books in a library and read those.

(2) ______ she finally went to study medicine, some men in her college didn't believe that she wanted to study. In 1849 she became the first woman in America to pass all the exams she needed to be a **(3)** ______.

In 1868 she **(4)** ______ a college just for women. A year later she went back to England to teach medicine to women in London. Today, you can read a book about her life **(5)** ______ how she helped many women become doctors in the nineteenth **(6)** ______.

EXAM TIP! Read the text **once** to understand what it's about. Read it **again** to choose the best answer. Then, read it **again** to check your answers.

5 Look at some answers to Activity 4. Are any of the answers wrong? Why/Why not?

1	A	study	**(B)**	studied	C	studio
2	A	Who	**(B)**	When	C	Where
3	A	doctor	B	medicine	**(C)**	bandage
4	A	open	B	opened	**(C)**	opening
5	**(A)**	but	B	because	C	and
6	A	century	B	months	**(C)**	years

1 2.08 **Listen.** Who's talking?

1 two friends
2
3
4
5
6

2 2.09 **Read the instructions and the options A, B and C.** What do you think the question is? Listen and check.

You hear a student talking about a film she watched on TV. What … ?

A an operation
B a king
C a queen

3 2.10 **Listen again.** Is the answer correct?

4 **Read the questions.** What are the key words?

1 Who did the girl watch the film with?
   A her mum B her mum and her cousin
2 The film about a magic queen was …
   A a history film. B a cartoon.
3 Which film did the girl want to see?
   A the film about an operation B a film about a king
4 Which film did they watch?
   A the cartoon B the history film

EXAM TIP! Read the question and options **carefully** before you listen. Think about the situation the person is in and **circle** any **key words**. Then think about similar words you might hear.

5 2.11 **Look again at the questions in Activity 4. Listen and choose the correct answer.**

6 2.12 **Listen and choose the correct answer.**

1 What did the woman buy for her grandson?
A a wallet B a football C a scooter

1 Choose the correct answer.

1 How long have you felt ill for?

A Since the accident. B For the accident.

2 What's wrong?

A I'm injuring my ankle. B I've injured my ankle.

3 Is your arm broken?

A I don't know. It's been painful since I fell off my bike.

B I don't know. It is painful since I fell off my bike.

4 How long have you had that cut?

A Three days ago. B For three days.

5 How long have you been a patient here?

A Last Tuesday. B Since last Tuesday.

2 Read the diary entry. Choose the correct answer.

15th August

Dear Diary,

Dizzy and I are feeling better now. We're having a special day together tomorrow to celebrate. In the morning I'm (1) ______ Dizzy for a haircut and a bath at the pet shop. I might buy her a new toy too. At 1 pm, (2) ______ meeting Carl and his dog, Floppy. Carl is my best friend and Floppy is Dizzy's best friend! Then, in the afternoon, my (3) ______ driving us to the hills again. We're (4) ______ walking and swimming – but I hope we (5) ______ going to the vet again!

	A		B		C	
1	A	take	B	taking	C	took
2	A	we're	B	we	C	we'll
3	A	aunt	B	aunt are	C	aunt's
4	A	go	B	going	C	to go
5	A	don't	B	not	C	aren't

3 Choose ten words from this unit. Record the words using the steps below.

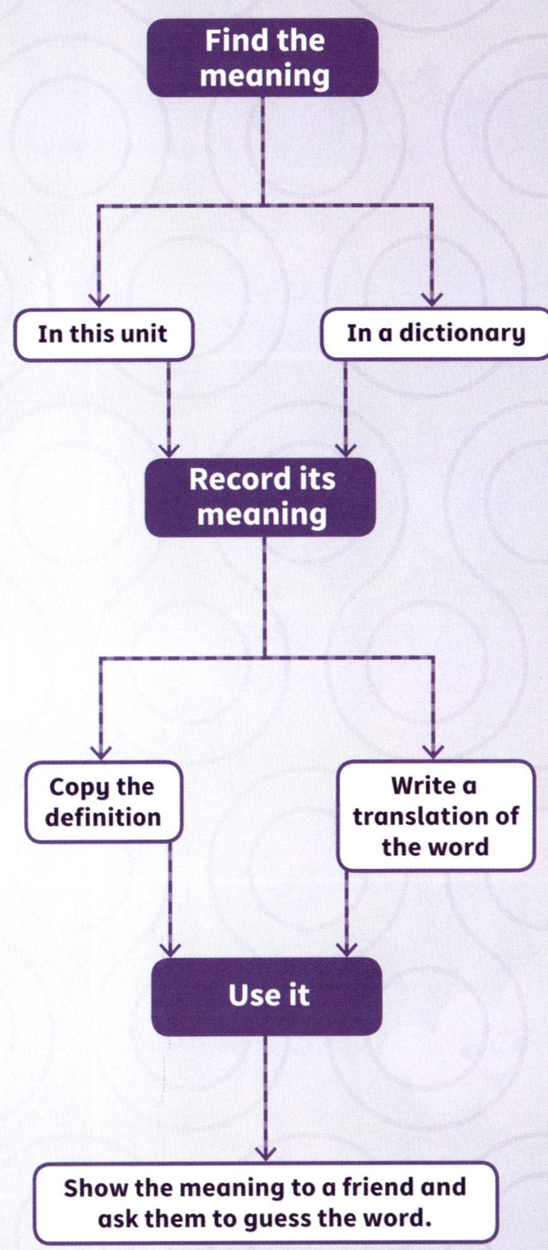

Mission in action!

Present what you have found out about emergency services.

In England, if you call 999, someone will probably answer the phone in five seconds.

5 Fun foods

Mission **Take part in a cooking competition**

1. Find out about food in different countries.
2. Choose a country and food. Plan how to make it.
★ Present your country and food. Choose a winner.

What food can you see? Choose three things that you'd like to eat.

Watch the video. How many chillies does Jim eat?

1 **Match the shopping lists (A–C) to the correct shopping baskets below.** Then say the food that is in each basket.

A
Broccoli
Salmon
Chillies

B
Garlic
Lamb
Herbs
Mushrooms

C
Cabbage
Steak
Onions
Oil

2 2.13 **Listen, point and say the numbers.**

Broccoli

Number 5

3 **Draw three foods from Activity 1 and hide your pictures.** Then guess which food your partner has.

Have you got something green?

Yes, I have.

Is it a vegetable?

Yes, it is.

You've got broccoli!

4 **Play 'I went to the supermarket and bought …'.**

1 **Look at the pictures in Activity 3.** Answer the questions.

- Which food can you see in the pictures?
- What's your favourite vegetable?

2 2.14 **Listen to five conversations.** How many times do you hear the word 'broccoli'?

3 2.15 **Listen again.** Choose the correct picture.

1  What's Claire's favourite dinner?

______

A B C

2  What would Mum like to have for dinner?

______

A B C

3  Which vegetable doesn't Emma like?

______

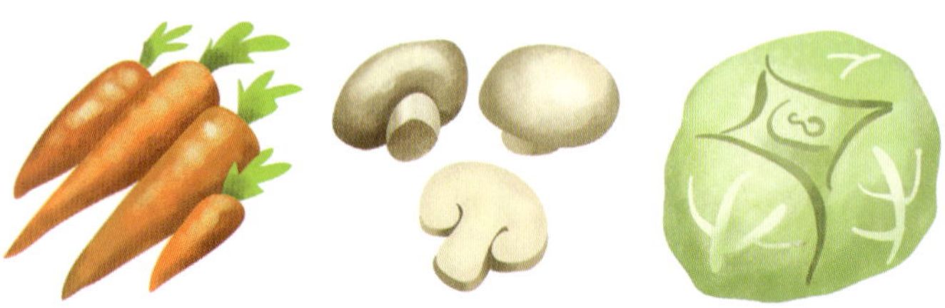

A B C

4  Which carrots would Karen prefer?

______

A B C

5  Which food can't Tom eat?

______

A B C

EXAM TIP! Try to answer as many questions as you can the first time you listen. **Check your answers** and do any missing answers when you listen to it the second time.

4 **Can you solve Claire's problem?** Think of a meal everyone at Claire's party can eat and write a menu.

Grammar look: *rather* and *prefer*

Karen: 'I prefer carrots to broccoli.'

1 What does Karen like more? **carrots / broccoli**

2 Which of the words could you add to the first sentence? **at the party / always**

Mum: 'I'd rather have salmon.'

3 What would Mum prefer to eat? **salmon / broccoli**

4 Which of the words can you add to Mum's answer? **at the party / always**

Tom: 'I'd prefer to have mushrooms.'

5 Which word is followed by the *to*-infinitive verb form (e.g. *to go, to have, to eat*)? **rather / prefer**

6 Which word is followed by the infinitive verb form without *to* (e.g. *go, have, eat*)? **rather / prefer**

We use *would rather* and *prefer* to say that we want or like one thing more than another thing.

page 123

1 **In pairs, ask and answer the questions.** Use your own ideas.

1 Do you prefer steak or salmon?
2 Do you prefer … or …?
3 For lunch tomorrow, would you prefer to … or …?
4 Do … or …?
5 …, would you …?
6 For dinner tonight, would you rather have broccoli or mushrooms?

2 **Choose one question from Activity 1 and ask your class.** Draw and write about the results.

Would my class rather have cake or jelly for dinner tonight?

I asked my class: 'Would you prefer cake or jelly for dinner tonight?' 12 people said they'd prefer cake. 15 people said they'd prefer jelly.

EXAM TIP! If you don't understand something remember to use these useful phrases:

Could you repeat that, please?

Pardon?

I'm sorry, I don't understand.

Mission Stage 1

Find out about food in different countries.

1 **Read Jim's blog quickly.** Which ingredients do you need for each dish?

Jim's Big Blog

*From **roast** chicken to **boiled** potatoes, Jenny and I love food (maybe because our dad's a chef.) Last week we asked three of our dad's friends how to make some awesome dishes. Enjoy!*

How was it made?!?

How was this ice cream sandwich made?

This sandwich wasn't made from bread! It was made from two cookies and some ice cream. It's an awesome dessert.

First, I got a round pot of ice cream and **cut** it into four pieces. Then I put each slice of ice cream onto a big cookie. Finally, I put another cookie on top. It was soooooooooooooo delicious!

(If you REALLY love sugar, you can melt some chocolate in a bowl over a **saucepan** and pour it onto your finished sandwich!)

– LittleLolz

How was this egg made?

Well, I think everyone knows how to **fry** an egg. You just break it and put it into a hot **frying pan** with some oil. This egg was fried like all others. But I used one little trick.

Before I put the egg in the pan, I **sliced** a large onion with a knife. Then, I took the largest ring of the onion and added it to the frying pan. Next, I put the egg into the onion ring to cook. That's how the egg was cooked in a circle. The last thing I did was make sure the egg looked happy!

– CookEggcellent

How were these caterpillars made?

Don't worry, these aren't real caterpillars! And they're very easy to make too, so they're perfect if you like healthy snacks.

To make a caterpillar, first, put six grapes on a stick and add eyes. Then, put the caterpillars in a **dish** in the freezer. I waited for about an hour (I put on the **kettle** and made myself a cup of tea) and the caterpillars were ready!

I took the caterpillars to a picnic and my friends said they were delicious. In fact, they were so popular that they were finished before I tried one!

– Pocco911

2 **Match the pictures to the words in bold in the blog.**

Number 1 is 'slice'.

1 
2 
3 
4 
5 
6 
7 
8 
9 

3 2.16 **What are the answers to the riddles?** Listen. Then write your own.

4 **Choose one of the dishes from the text above.** Draw pictures to show how it was made.

Grammar look: the passive (past simple)

'This sandwich wasn't made from bread. It was made from two cookies and some ice cream.'

1 Are the sentences active or passive? **active** / **passive**

2 When is the sentence talking about? **the past** / **the present**

3 How is the passive made (in the past simple)?
was **or** ***wasn't*** **+ past participle** (e.g. *made*, *written*, *had*) /
was **or** ***wasn't*** **+ infinitive** (e.g. *to make*, *to write*, *to have*)

We use the passive when we don't know who does something or when it isn't important who does it.

page 123

1 2.17 **PRONUNCIATION Listen and repeat.** page 119

2 How were the chocolate dishes made? Write a sentence for each picture (1–8).

1 

Some chocolate | melt | in a bowl over a saucepan

2 

Chocolate circles | make | on a tray

3 

Some balloons | fill | with air

4 

The balloons | dip | into chocolate

5 

The balloons | put | on the chocolate circles

6 

The balloons | leave | until they were hard

7 

Holes | made | in the balloons

8 

The chocolate dishes | fill | with fruit

3 Cover the sentences in Activity 2. Try to remember each one.

Some chocolate was melted in a bowl!

Mission Stage 2

Choose a country and food. Plan how to make it.

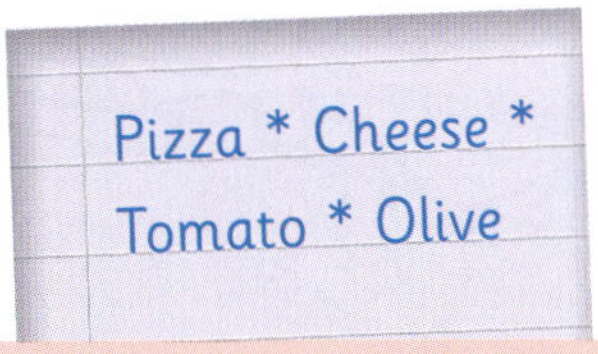

1 **Have you read any diaries?** What did you think of them? Do you write, or would you like to write, a diary of your own?

2.19

The very, very interesting diary of Juana Sánchez

Monday

My parents think the show is brilliant. It's the only thing they talk about. 'Oh, Juana,' Mum said at breakfast. 'Your brother's got 63,000 subscribers to his channel!' 'Oh, Juana,' Dad said at dinner. 'Your brother's going to be world famous.' 'My last video was watched 1,000,000 times, Juana,' Carlos said. 'Have you seen the show yet?' No, I haven't. I'd rather clean my granddad's shoes with an old toothbrush.

The show's on YouTube. It's the only thing he talks about. 'Oh, Juana,' he said after dinner when I was washing up his dirty plate. 'I made chilli today. My fans loved it!'

Wednesday

Before dinner, I asked Carlos to help me lay the table. 'Well, Juana,' he said, 'I'm an Internet star now, you know, and I haven't got time to lay the table. I've got my next show to think about.'

I'm going to ask Mum if we can change him for a cat.

Friday

I was tired after school and wanted to relax on the sofa, but Carlos kept talking about his next show. 'On Sunday morning I'm going to do my new recipe for spaghetti bolognese. All I need is … .' The only way I could get him to stop talking was to say, 'Carlos, on Sunday, I'm going to watch your show.'

Saturday

I had to help Dad in the garden this morning. I hate gardening. There are worms everywhere – long, thin worms. I don't like worms, but they gave me an idea …

Sunday

Carlos was like a four-year-old at a birthday party today. 'I'm so happy you're going to watch my show,' he said. 'I've got everything ready – the onions, the garlic, the herbs, the spaghetti. Now, time for my shower.' Carlos always has a shower before his shows. 'I must look my best for my fans!' he says. When he was in the bathroom, I went into the kitchen, took the spaghetti out of the pot, and put something else in.

'Right, let's go!' said Carlos when he came back into the kitchen. 'Mum and Dad usually turn the camera on for me, Juana, but you can do it today. Are you ready? Let me get in position. OK. Press the button … now. Good morning, friends!. Today I'm going to show you how to make spaghetti bolognese. Now, in this pot I've already put the … worms! Arghhhhhhhhhhhhh!'

OK, it wasn't the nicest thing to do. But more people have watched this video than any of his other ones! And I'm sure he'll talk to me again – one day.

2 In pairs, role play a conversation. Imagine you are Juana and Carlos.

STUDENT A You are Carlos. You are very angry with Juana. You don't understand why she played a trick on you.

STUDENT B You are Juana. You want to say sorry to Carlos. You know you did the wrong thing, but you'd like him to understand that he shouldn't talk about himself all the time and that he should ask other people about their interests.

I'm very angry with you, Juana. My show is very important to me. Why did you put worms in my pot?

I'm very sorry, Carlos. But why do you talk about your show all the time?

1 **Read the text and look at the photos. What food groups do the foods belong to? Which nutrients do they give us? Use the words in the boxes.**

Food groups: grains, cereals and potatoes | meat, fish, nuts and beans | dairy | fruits and vegetables | fats and oils

Nutrients: calcium | vitamins and minerals | fats | proteins | carbohydrates

Superfoods?

It's important to eat a balanced diet and different foods give us different nutrients. Proteins make our muscles strong. Calcium is good for our teeth and bones and carbohydrates give us energy to exercise and play in the day.

Some foods have more nutrients than others but does this make them superfoods? Most doctors think that we shouldn't call them 'superfoods' but 'super diets' – this means we should eat a healthy, balanced diet with lots of fruit, vegetables and wholegrain foods.

Here are some foods that aren't super, but have lots of vitamins that are very good for you:

Blueberries have got vitamins K and C in them as well as other nutrients. Some people think that blueberries can protect us from heart problems and improve our memory. Try adding them to your breakfast cereal or have them for a snack.

Oily fish like salmon or sardines have got vitamin D, protein and some B vitamins. Oily fish has also got good fat in it. If you eat oily fish two or more times a week it keeps your eyes and your bones healthy.

Broccoli has got lots of vitamins, calcium and fibre in it! It's a vegetable that you can eat in salads, soups and with meat and fish.

Some people think that dark chocolate is good for us, but like any food, you shouldn't eat lots of it. A little bit of dark chocolate is better than milk chocolate, but if you eat it too much, it's an unhealthy choice.

2 2.20 **Listen and read the text again.** Match the sentence halves.

1 Proteins are good for
2 Calcium is good for
3 We should eat
4 Blueberries have got
5 Oily fish
6 Broccoli
7 You shouldn't eat

A has got vitamin D in it.
B has lots of fibre in it.
C too much chocolate.
D vitamin K in them.
E a healthy balanced diet.
F your teeth and bones.
G your muscles.

3 **In pairs, talk about food you prefer. Do you eat any 'superfoods'?**

I'd rather eat cereal for breakfast than toast.

I prefer blueberries to strawberries.

1 Read and answer the questions.

1 What can you do on a cooking tour?

2 Would you like to go on one? Why/Why not?

2 Read the question. Think of some places Tim may have visited.

You will hear Tim talking to a friend about a cooking tour with his dad. What day did he visit the places?

Where did Tim go?

The museum.

A shopping centre.

3 2.21 Listen to the conversation. Write two places you hear for each day.

1 Tuesday ....
2 Wednesday ....
3 Thursday ....
4 Friday ....
5 Saturday ....

4 2.22 Listen again and choose the correct answer.

Days

1 Tuesday ......
2 Wednesday ......
3 Thursday ......
4 Friday ......
5 Saturday ......

Places

A apartment
B train station
C café
D museum
E TV studio
F town hall
G park
H farm

EXAM TIP!
Remember, sometimes you hear **two options**. Listen carefully for words that might mean that one option isn't correct. For example:

- no
- didn't
- weren't

1 Which phrases in the box are useful for starting a story?

One day … Finally, Dear Sally, Then, Lots of love, After that, Last week
Thanks for your email, Next, Because of this, In the end, Yesterday,

2 Look at picture A and write a sentence. Use a phrase from the box in Activity 1.

3 Which of the sentences is the best first line for this story? Why?

1 One day a man drinks an orange juice. ______________________

2 Tony likes cooking. ______________________

3 Last week John went to have dinner at a restaurant. ______________________

4 Look at the rest of the story. Choose a phrase and finish the sentences.

Then/Next ______________________

Finally/In the end ______________________

5 Read two students' answers. In pairs, talk about which story is better and why.

In the second story, the people have names.

1

a man one day goes to eat in ristorant. He's look his phone. A girl enters. She is with woman. The girls present is beutifull People is happy.

2

One day, John went to have dinner at Tony's restaurant. He was waiting for someone and he felt worried. Then his daughter Betty arrived with her mum. Betty opened her beautiful present and Tony gave her a necklace. It was a really fun evening.

EXAM TIP! Remember to write about **all three** pictures. Your story should have a beginning, a middle and an end.

1 Choose the correct words to complete the sentences.

1. I always **prefer** / **rather** broccoli to mushrooms.
2. At the picnic, I'd **prefer** / **rather** have sandwiches than lamb and cabbage.
3. I'd rather **have** / **to have** onion sauce, please.
4. I'd prefer **to eat** / **eat** garlic than onion.
5. For lunch today, **I'd** / **I** prefer to have steak than salmon.
6. **We'd** / **We** always prefer food with lots of chilli in it.

2 Complete the text. Use the words in brackets and the past passive.

Last week, I went to a restaurant for my grandma's birthday. The restaurant was very strange. The walls **(1)** __________ (decorate) with vegetables and the waiters **(2)** __________ (dress) as carrots!

First, I had broccoli soup. It **(3)** __________ (cook) with chilli and onion so it was delicious – but very spicy. Next, I had lamb with vegetables. The lamb **(4)** __________ (roast) perfectly and the vegetables were brilliant too. They **(5)** __________ (fry) with some lovely herbs. Finally, for dessert, I had an apple that **(6)** __________ (slice) so it looked like a bird!

3 Choose ten words from this unit. Record the words using the steps below.

Find the meaning
- In this unit
- In an online recipe

Record the example
- Replace the word with a picture
- Leave a space for your word

Use it

Challenge a friend to find the right word to complete your sentence.

Mission in action!

Present your country and food. Choose a winner!

6 Environmentally friendly

1

2

3

4

5

6

7

8

9

Mission Share ideas to protect the environment

1. Find environmentally friendly items at home.
2. Find out about how your items are environmentally friendly. Interview each other.

★ Present your ideas to protect your environment.

What can you see in the pictures? Which objects have been recycled?

Watch the video. What does Jenny make from her old jeans?

1 2.23 **Listen and point to the things in Ela's house.** Say the numbers.

Above the stairs is a cool bulb.

Number 2

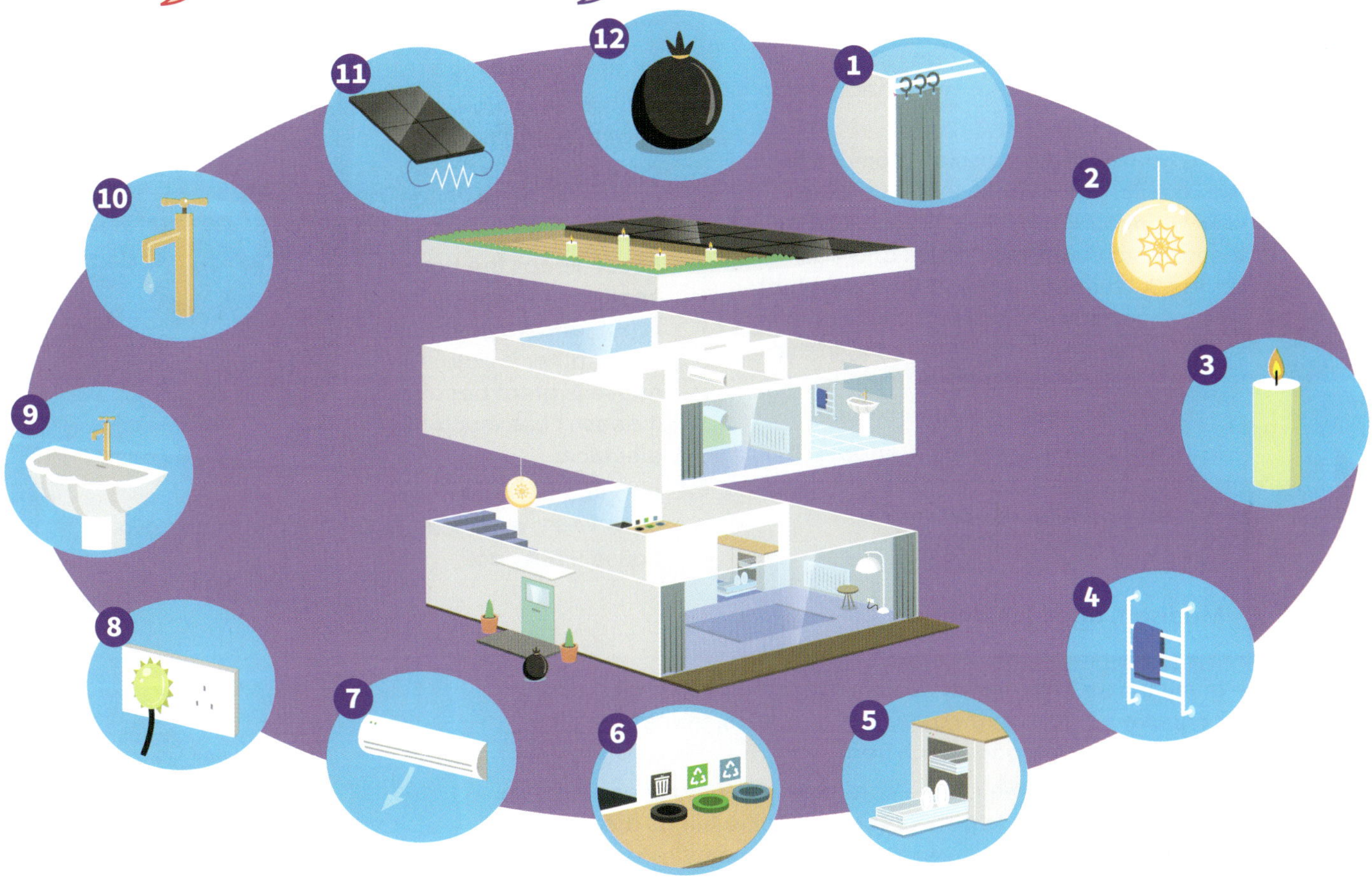

2 **In pairs, use the words in the box to check the things (1–12) in the picture.**

curtain	dustbin	tap	electricity	rubbish	sink
air conditioning	dishwasher	candle	plug	bulb	heating

What's number 1?

Curtain.

3 **Complete the diagram with the words from Activity 2.**

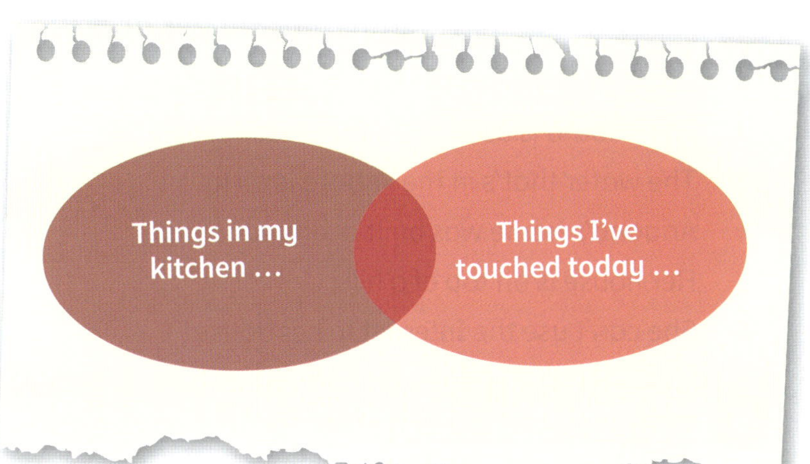

4 **In pairs, share your diagrams.** What are three differences?

I've touched a dustbin today but Clara hasn't.

Riku, aged 9, Japan

Most people aren't surprised that I don't have a dishwasher. But when I say that fish clean my dishes for me, many people don't believe me!

In my garden there's a small room, called the kabata. In the room, there's a lot of water from our town's river. My family use the water to clean vegetables and wash dishes. A little food falls off the bowls that we wash – but that's OK because there are lots of fish living in the water, and the fish eat the food. The fish keep the water clean!

After the water comes to my kabata, it goes into the river or onto farms. A kabata is a great way to save water!

Ariadna, aged 10, Spain

There isn't heating or air conditioning in my house.

I live in a traditional cave house – a house that's built inside a hill. The ground around the house keeps the house cool when the weather is hot, and warm when the weather is cold. My house is great because it doesn't use much electricity.

People think that I don't have Wi-Fi, electricity or even water in my cave house – but I do!

Madison, aged 11, Canada

In my house there isn't a dustbin. My family don't need one because we don't throw away much rubbish. In fact, we only throw away a few bags each year.

How do we do it? Well, we're careful when we go shopping – we take our own bags to put our food in. Some things are always wrapped in plastic, but we try not to buy them. Instead, we buy lots of fresh fruit and vegetables.

Finally, when we have a little rubbish, we try to use it. I've made a lot of cool things from plastic bottles!

1 **Read the article for 60 seconds. Which item *doesn't* each child have in their house?**

2 **Read the article again and say *yes* or *no*.**

1 Riku's kabata is in the kitchen of their home.
2 The kabata is used to do the washing up.
3 The water that's in the kabata is dirty.
4 Ariadna's home was built a long time ago.
5 Her house is on top of a hill.
6 She can't use the Internet in her house.
7 Madison's family throw away less rubbish than most people.
8 Her family don't buy things in plastic bottles, boxes or bags.
9 She often recycles things by using them in a new way.

3 **Why is each house better for the environment than normal houses? Which would you like to live in?**

In Riku's house they save water. It's bad for the environment to use too much water because …

Grammar look: *a lot of, lots of, a few, a little, many, much*

'There's a lot of water from our town's river.'
'There are lots of fish living in the water.'
'Many people don't believe me.'

'My house doesn't use much electricity.'
'When we have a little rubbish, we try to use it.'
'We only throw away a few bags each year.'

1. *Lots of* and *a lot of* / *A little* means 'a large amount of' something (e.g. money, time, food) or number of something (e.g. clothes, people, cars).
2. *Many* / *Much* means 'a large amount of' something (e.g. money, time, food). It's usually used in negative sentences and questions.
3. *Many* / *Much* means 'a large number of' something (e.g. clothes, people, cars). It's usually used in negative sentences and questions.
4. *Lots of* and *a lot of* / *A little* means 'a small amount of something' (e.g. money, time, food).
5. *A few* / *Many* means 'a small number of' something (e.g. clothes, people, cars).

page 124

1 2.24 **PRONUNCIATION Listen and repeat.** page 119

2 **Look at the three pictures and write the story.** Write 35 words or more, using some of the words in the box.

a lot of	lots	a few	a little	many	much

EXAM TIP! When you've finished writing, **read your text again** and check the grammar and spelling.

Did you know?

We use more than 100,000,000* bottles every day. That's the same weight as six Statues of Liberty. Many of these bottles aren't recycled and cause problems for the environment.

*one-hundred million

3 **Read your story to a small group.** Whose story do you like best?

Mission Stage 1

Find environmentally friendly items at home.

1 2.27 **Listen to the podcast.** Who always uses recycled paper? ______________

A

B

C

D

E

F

G

H

I

J

2 2.28 **Match the words (1–10) to the pictures (A–J). Listen and check.**

1	recycle	☐	6	petrol	☐
2	area	☐	7	path	☐
3	litter	☐	8	pollution	☐
4	traffic jams	☐	9	gas	☐
5	public transport	☐	10	rainforest	☐

3 2.29 **Listen again.** Which time was better for the sentences (1–6)?

	Now	When Grandma was young
1 People are better at recycling.	✓	
2 People make less rubbish.		
3 People are better at throwing away their litter.		
4 The air is cleaner.		
5 People use less gas and electricity.		
6 People save gas and electricity.		
TOTAL:		

4 **When do you think life was better for the environment?** Discuss and vote.

Grammar look: tag questions

\+ –

'Everyone recycles a lot, don't they?'

– +

'You couldn't recycle, could you?'

'Since you started school you've travelled by car, haven't you?'

'The air was cleaner then, wasn't it?'

Tag questions change statements into questions. They're often used to check that someone agrees with us.

1 When the first part of the sentence is positive, the tag question is **positive** / **negative**.

2 When the first part of the sentence is negative, the tag question is **positive** / **negative**.

3 If the first part of the sentence has an auxiliary verb (e.g. *be*, *have*, *can* etc.), you use the **the same** / **a different** auxiliary verb in the tag question.

4 If the first part of the sentence doesn't have an auxiliary verb, we use ***is*, *are* or *was*** / ***do*, *does* or *did*** in the tag question.

page 124

1 Match the sentences (1–6) to the correct tag questions (A–F).

1	Your name's Glenda,	A	wasn't it?
2	You live in London,	B	isn't it?
3	Your house was built a long time ago,	C	can you?
4	You don't have a dishwasher,	D	have you?
5	You haven't been to the rainforest,	E	don't you?
6	You can't use public transport,	F	do you?

2 **Invent a character.** Ask and answer the questions from Activity 1.

Your name's Glenda, isn't it?

No, my name's Holly Wood. And I love American films!

Mission Stage 2

Find out about how your items are environmentally friendly. Interview each other.

1 **Look at the pictures.** Where do you think the story takes place? What animals can you see?

2.30

The fall of a Mayan city

The Mayan king looked down at the city from his palace. He felt very sad. He could remember the brightly coloured pyramids and temples; the exotic gardens full of jaguars, pumas and parrots and the buzzing street markets with delicious food from all over his empire. It was one of the great wonders of the world. But now the city was silent and empty. And why was this …?

Many years before, when the king was looking for somewhere to live, he saw a big beautiful ceiba tree in the heart of the tropical rainforest. He decided that it was the perfect place to make his home. Just as he was about to leave an old man appeared from behind the tree.

'We have always looked after the rainforest and you must too,' he said. 'Don't chop down the trees! Build your city somewhere else!' And he disappeared into the forest again.

But the king ignored the old man's advice. 'He's just a crazy old man,' he thought to himself. And he built his city nearby.

As the king and his people became richer and more powerful the city grew and grew. People needed more space to build their houses and grow their corn. So they chopped down more and more trees from the rainforest. Everything seemed perfect, until one day things started to change. At first it didn't rain as much as it usually did and the rivers became smaller and smaller. Then it stopped raining and the rivers dried up. The corn in the fields and the vegetables in the gardens dried up, too. With little food and water, the people started to leave the city. The king was very worried.

'What can I do?' he asked his advisors.

None of them could give him an answer. Then he remembered the old man he met in the forest. He went back and looked for the tall ceiba tree. Eventually he found it but now it was standing alone in the middle of a desert. He sat under its branches in the shade.

Suddenly, the same old man came out from behind the tree.

'Look what you've done,' said the old man.

The king fell to his knees and asked, 'Please tell me – what should I do?'

'Well there is a solution but it will take many, many years,'the old man said. This time, the king listened carefully to every word.

'If you plant two trees for every one you chopped down then maybe the rain will return and maybe the rivers, the plants, the birds and the animals will come back,' the old man said, and suddenly disappeared, just like before.

Quickly, the king ordered his people to plant trees where there was now desert. Slowly but surely, as the years passed, the trees grew, the rain came back and the rainforest filled with life again. First the animals and birds returned and then the people. The king was delighted. Before he died he made sure that the ceiba tree was always protected, so that his people would look after the rainforest.

2 In pairs, talk about the questions.

1. What happened in the story when the people cut down too many trees in the rainforest? Why did this happen?
2. How did they fix the problem?
3. Do you think the king was responsible for what happened?

Cross-curricular

1 **Look at the pictures.** What living and non-living things can you see in them?

2 2.31 **Listen and read the text about urban ecosystems.** Find the animals – do you know them all?

Where we live

An ecosystem is all of the living and non-living things that are in an area. Living things include all of the plants and animals and non-living things are the rocks, water, soil and sand. Examples of ecosystems are an ocean, a rainforest, a pond, a desert, a river, grassland or an urban ecosystem.

As cities and towns get bigger, other ecosystems get smaller. This means that a lot of animals don't have anywhere to live and so they start to come into cities and towns to look for food and somewhere to sleep. Usually these are small animals like mice, rats and foxes, but in some cities there are some very unusual animals:

Leopards in Mumbai

Mumbai is a very big city and about 24 million people live there. It also has a big park called the Gandhi National Park and this is where leopards and other animals live. But as the city gets bigger, the leopards are losing their homes. So, the leopards often come into town to look for food. Some people are trying to find a different place for the leopards but the animals don't like moving to different places. So for now, people and leopards have to try and live together.

Peregrine falcons in New York

Peregrine falcons usually live near the beach but when they started to die, people in New York decided to help them live in the city. Now New York has more peregrine falcons than any other city in the world. That's amazing, isn't it? They like living in the city because there are lots of high places to make their nests where they are safe and there is a lot of food to eat too. The people of New York and the birds live happily together.

Did you know?

Birds sing louder in cities. This is so that they can be heard by other birds – they are talking!

3 **Read the text again and in pairs, answer the questions.**

1. How have humans changed natural ecosystems?
2. Should the leopards move to a different home?
3. What problems do you think wild animals have when they live in a city?
4. What problems do you think people have when wild animals come into a city?

1 **Watch the video to see an example of Speaking Part 2.**

2 **Read the question and two answers.** Which answer is better? Why?

Do you like these different homes?

Yes, I do.

No, I don't because this one is very small and this one hasn't got any curtains.

3 **Look at these pictures.** Think of one thing to say about each home.

4 **Choose an adjective and make a question.** Ask and answer the questions.

fun boring
interesting
expensive noisy

Do you think a beach house is … ?

Do you think a tree house is … ?

Do you think a castle is … ?

Do you think a flat is … ?

Do you think a beach house is fun?

Yes, I do. It's fun because …

5 **Look at the pictures in Activity 3 again.** Ask and answer.

Which of these homes do you like best? Why?

I like the beach houses best because …

6 **Look at the questions.** Choose an answer and finish the sentences with your own ideas.

Now, would you prefer to live in the town or the countryside? Why?

I think … because …

I prefer … because …

Which is more important? Living with heating or living with electricity?

It's more important to … because …

EXAM TIP! Practise giving your opinion to a friend. Remember to use **full sentences**.

1 Read the two example exam questions below. What does each person want to know?

Read the email from your British friend Emily.
Write an email to Emily and answer the questions.

From: Emily **To:**

It's my party on Friday but I need some help. Can you come to my garden after school finishes at 4:30 pm? Which food can you bring? What shall we tidy up?

Emily

Write 25–35 words.
Write the email on your answer sheet.

You recently joined a new afternoon club. Write a note to your English-speaking friend Linda. In your note:

- Tell her what you do at the club
- Say how much it costs
- Ask if your friend wants to go with you

Write 25–35 words.
Write the email on your answer sheet.

2 Look at the answers below. What can Costas and Federica do to improve their writing? Use the checklist.

Dear Emily,
Thanks for your message. I'm fine thanks. I know about your party and I can come at 4:30 on Friday. I can make and bring a very good Greek salad. I think we could tidy up the kitchen and the play area.
Bye,
Costas

Hi Sam,
I go to a nature club every Tuesday after school. We make instruments from wood. It's fun! It's only costs 2 euros every week.
See you tomorow,
Federica

EXAM TIP! To get a good mark, your writing must have **all three** things being asked for in the exam.

CHECKLIST

- [ ] Write to the person in the question.
- [ ] Write about the 3 things in the question.
- [ ] Write 25–35 words.
- [ ] Write on the answer sheet.

1 Read the text and choose the correct words.

Last week, our art class's project was to make something using recycled materials. At first, we didn't have **(1)** _____ ideas so we did some research on the Internet. Then I made a bag with **(2)** _____ old T-shirts. It's big so I can put **(3)** _____ my things in it. My friend, Anna, wanted to use **(4)** _____ old cardboard boxes. So she made a cool bookcase.

You can make amazing things with **(5)** _____ rubbish and it doesn't take **(6)** _____ time if you plan carefully and use your imagination.

	A	B	C
1	a lot of	many	a little
2	much	a little	a few
3	lots of	much	many
4	many	a lot of	a little
5	a little	much	a few
6	many	a few	much

3 Choose ten words from this unit. Record the words using the steps below.

Find the meaning
- In this unit
- In a dictionary

Record the example
- Draw the word
- Write similar words

Use it

Show the meaning of the word to a partner. Can they guess it?

2 Say a tag question for each sentence. Then match the questions (1–6) to the answers (A–F).

1 It's hot in here, _____?
2 We can recycle this plastic, _____?
3 There isn't a dustbin here, _____?
4 I shouldn't leave the tap on, _____?
5 We're going to be late, _____?
6 That petrol was expensive, _____?

A No, there's one outside though.
B Yes, the air conditioning's broken.
C Yes, we are. This traffic jam's awful!
D Yes, it was cheaper at the other petrol station last week.
E Yes, put it in the blue bin.
F No, it wastes a lot of water.

If my family and I put new bins in our house, we can recycle more plastic.

Mission in action!

Present your ideas to protect your environment.

Review • • • Units 4–6

1 **Watch the video and do the quiz.**

2 **Complete the sentences using *for* or *since*.**

1 The new path has been open ________ three weeks.

2 My family have recycled everything ________ we moved to our new house.

3 This traffic jam has stopped us ________ an hour!

4 I've picked up the litter in the picnic area every day ________ a month.

5 I've been worried about the rainforest ________ I watched a TV program about it.

6 I've taken public transport to school ________ I started going there.

3 **Complete the sentences.** Use the words in brackets and the present continuous.

Next Monday, I'm not going to work. At 9 am, **(1)** ________ (**I/get up**) and boiling myself an egg for breakfast. At 10 am, **(2)** ________ (**I/drive**) to the mountains and going fishing. **(3)** ________ (**I/take**) a frying pan. If I catch a fish, I'll make a fire and fry it for my lunch. After lunch, **(4)** ________ (**I/not/answer**) the phone because I want to lie down and rest. Then, at 8 pm, I'm going to the cinema with my son. **(5)** ________ (**We/watch**) *Spiderman*.

4 **Write about your day tomorrow.** Write 25–35 words.

5 **Complete the sentences.** Use the words in the box.

turn on	prefers (x2)	to drink	would rather (x2)

1 John ________ to have candles on his hamster's birthday cake.

2 Jane ________ get blue penguin curtains than get ones with aliens.

3 My dad ________ use a dishwasher than wash up in the sink.

4 My sister ________ hotel rooms with air-conditioning.

5 Judy prefers ________ tap water to bottled water.

6 Joshua would rather ________ the air conditioning than take off his favourite jumper.

6 2.32 **Listen.** Write the sentences.

1

2

3

4

7 Find the mistakes. Write the correct sentences.

1 I spend much money on clothes.

____

2 In my town you can go to the museum, the beach and a lot other beautiful places.

____

3 I like it alot.

____

4 I haven't got much DVDs.

____

5 I don't have much things to do today.

____

6 People spend lot of time in front of the TV.

____

8 Read the situations and complete the tag questions.

1 You are at a restaurant with your family. The salmon is very expensive. What do you say?
The salmon is very expensive, isn't it?

2 You don't have enough onions for your recipe. You want to know if your friend has a spare one. What do you say?
You haven't _______________

3 Your friend is coming to your house for dinner. You think she doesn't like broccoli but you want to check. What do you say?
You don't like _______________

4 You think your uncle can eat mushrooms but you want to check with your mum. What do you say?
My uncle can _______________

5 You think your friend goes to school by bus. What do you say?
You travel _______________

9 Choose and complete two of the challenges.

CHALLENGE 1
Say an ingredient, cooking verb or piece of cooking equipment that starts with each of the following letters:
F-R-U-I-T S-A-L-A-D

CHALLENGE 2
Look at Unit 4. Find:
- seven things that can make you feel bad.
- three things that can make you feel better.
- a part of your body.

CHALLENGE 3
Look at the pictures of objects on pages 67 and 70. Write a list of 10 objects that you have in your home and 5 objects that you don't have.

7 Feeling it

1

2

3

4

5

6

7

8

9

How would you feel in each picture? When have you felt like this?

Watch the video. What makes Jim feel annoyed?

Mission Make a 'feelings wheel'

1. Brainstorm different emotions you feel.
2. Make a list of tips for feeling better.

★ Make a feelings wheel with real suggestions.

1 **Read the poster.** Match the definitions (1–11) to the words in bold.

A I feel **relaxed** …
- when I'm at home with my cats.
- at school when I'm with my friends.

B I feel **miserable** …
- when I'm ill.
- when it rains for days and days. I like sunny weather!

C I feel **annoyed** …
- with Sam for telling Marie my secret.
- about the rain today. I want to ride my bike.

D I feel **amazed** …
- when I go to watch fireworks.
- when I see rainbows.

E I feel **positive** …
- about my team this season. (I think we'll win the league!)
- about my friends. I love you all!

F I feel **worried** …
- because I don't have a T-shirt for P.E. Can anyone lend me one?
- about going to the dentist next week.

G I feel **negative** …
- about my project – I need to try harder.
- when I can't answer a question in maths.

H I feel **satisfied** …
- when I finish some work at school and I know I've tried my best.
- after I've eaten a huge pizza!

I I feel **embarrassed** …
- when I speak in front of other people.
- when my phone rings in the library!!!!

J I feel **interested** …
- in dolphins. Did you know that some dolphins only have eight teeth but others have 250?
- in recycling old clothes. Who wants to learn sewing with me?

K I feel **bored** …
- when my friends play computer games.
- when I'm sitting in the car. But it's great to arrive at the beach or my cousin's house!

1 only thinking of the bad side of something ☐
2 full of hope ☐
3 free of worries ☐
4 pleased because you have what you wanted ☐
5 very unhappy ☐
6 unhappy and tired because something isn't interesting ☐
7 very surprised ☐
8 unhappy and thinking about your problems ☐
9 a bit angry ☐
10 shy ☐
11 wanting to read about, talk about or learn more about something ☐

2 **Complete five of the *I feel …* sentences from Activity 1 so that they are true for you.**

I feel relaxed when I'm at home watching TV.

3 3.02 **PRONUNCIATION**
Listen and repeat.

page 119

1 **Read Jim's blog quickly.** What problems do you think the people have?

Jim's Big Blog

This week we asked our friends if we could help with any of their problems. Here's what we wrote!

Helping our friends

Hello,

I love your blog! You always have interesting ideas to write about.

How can I think of ideas for my blog? I often sit in my room thinking until I feel miserable. Please help!

Thanks, Kyo_hearts

We find it hard to think of ideas for our blog, too. We have to work really hard!

The best way to have a few good ideas is to have lots of ideas. You should write a long list of things you're interested in. You needn't worry if some of your ideas aren't very good and you don't have to spend more than five or ten minutes writing either. When you've finished the list you can use the best ideas in your blog.

Jim

Hi Kyo_hearts,

You ought to write about something you love. It doesn't matter if your blog's popular or not. If you're blogging about what you love, then you'll love blogging.

Jenny

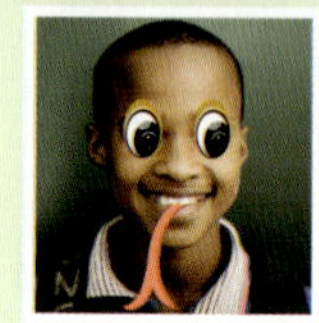

Hi,

I'd like a pet snake to love and look after, but my parents say that I can't. I ask them but they always say I have to wait until I'm older. I'm so annoyed with them. Do you think I should get one without telling them?

Florenville2025

I think you ought to understand your parents. Why don't they want you to have a snake? Maybe they're worried about how much it costs? Or maybe they're annoyed with you because you often ask them about it?

You shouldn't get a snake without telling your parents. You'll be too worried about them finding it.

Jim

Hi Florenville2025,

No! NO! NO! You **MUSTN'T** get a snake without telling your parents. You should try to be satisfied with what you have. You ought to get a plant if you want something to love and look after.

If your parents say you can't have a snake, you must listen to them!

Jenny

2 ☆ **Read the blog again.** Say which person ...

1 enjoyed reading Jim and Jenny's blog.
   A Kyo_hearts   B Florenville2025

2 thinks it is hard to have ideas to write about.
   A Jim   B Jenny

3 feels a bit angry with his parents.
   A Jenny   B Florenville2025

4 thinks that Florenville2025 won't feel relaxed if he gets a snake.
   A Jim   B Jenny

EXAM TIP! Make sure you know exactly which part of the text gives you the answer to the question. If it helps you, **underline the sentences** in the text which are useful.

3 **Who do you think gave the most useful advice?** What advice would you give?

Grammar look: *needn't, have to, should, ought to, must, mustn't*

'I have to wait until I'm older.'

'If your parents say you can't have a snake, you must listen to them!'

'You mustn't get a snake without telling your parents.'

'You needn't worry if some of your ideas aren't very good.'

'You don't have to spend more than five or ten minutes writing either.'

'You should try to be satisfied with what you have.'

'You ought to write about something you love.'

1 *Have to* and ***must*** / ***should*** have similar meanings. They're used when we don't choose to do something and someone else (like a parent, teacher or the police) chooses for us.

2 ***Ought to*** / ***Needn't*** and *don't have to* have similar meanings. They are used when we do not need to do something. Their meaning is different to *mustn't*. *Mustn't* is used when there is a rule about something you cannot do.

3 *Should* and ***ought to*** / ***mustn't*** have similar meanings. They are used when something is correct or a good thing to do. We can choose if we want to do these things.

page 125

1 **Read two more messages to Jim and Jenny.** Write three sentences to reply to each message. Use *needn't*, *have to*, *should*, *ought to*, *must* or *mustn't*.

1 I forgot my best friend's birthday last week and I didn't get him a card or say 'Happy Birthday'. I feel really miserable because of it. What should I do?

SnakeGoat

2 My friends want to go swimming in the river after school, but I'm worried about it. There's a big sign that says it's dangerous to swim. What should I do?

Lunchtime_Tam

2 **In pairs, share your ideas.** Which letter would you like to reply to?

I'd like to reply to Letter 1. I forgot my cousin's birthday once, so I know what SnakeGoat should do.

Mission Stage 1

Brainstorm different emotions you feel.

Nervous – if I have a test

Excited – seeing my friends

Interested – when we learn about science

1 3.04 **Listen. Where did the boy fall asleep?** ____________________

2 3.05 **Listen again and point to pictures 1–6.**

3 3.06 **Complete the sentences.** Use the words in the box. Listen and check.

breathe deeply	do exercise	go jogging	goes to the gym	look after her health	keep fit	reduce stress	recover	aching	diet

1 My mum said she was feeling worried because we're moving house so she wanted a way to __________ .
2 We go to the sports centre together to relax and __________ .
3 You can __________ there, like running or swimming.
4 When we __________ we wear special glasses. It feels like we're running away from a monster!
5 While my mum __________ to lift weights, there's a big swimming pool where I go to swim with sharks.
6 After we exercise, there are lovely places to sit and __________ .
7 There's a little pool that we sit in when we've got tired, __________ legs.
8 There's a garden on the roof. You can just sit, __________ and listen to the river.
9 They've only got healthy food. A good __________ is important – so they haven't got cake or ice cream.
10 My mum always says she wants to __________ better.

4 ☆ **In pairs, ask and answer the questions.**

1 What kinds of exercise do you like doing?
2 What do you do to look after your health?
3 What do you think are the best ways to reduce stress?

EXAM TIP! When you answer questions, use **full sentences** and try to say four things.

Grammar look: *such … that / so … that*

'It's so fun that my mum and I always laugh a lot!'
'It's such a relaxing place that I once fell asleep there!'

1 *So … that* and *such … that* are used for **surprising, strange or unusual / boring, uninteresting or normal** situations.
2 We use **so / such** with adjectives (e.g. *good, bad, boring*) or adverbs (e.g. *quickly, tiny*).
3 We use **so / such** with noun phrases (e.g. *an interesting person, a great cook*).

page 125

1 Complete the sentences. Use *so … that* or *such … that.*

1 I exercised for _such_ a long time _that_ my legs ached!
2 I felt ________ stressed ________ I couldn't sleep!
3 I was ________ embarrassed ________ my face was red!
4 I thought it was ________ a boring book ________ I didn't finish it!
5 I felt ________ annoyed ________ I walked away!
6 It was ________ a big sandwich ________ I couldn't eat it all!

2 Complete the sentences with your own ideas.

1 It was such a delicious cake that ________
2 The weather was so ________
3 The test was so difficult that ________
4 It was such a hot day that ________

3 Work in small groups. Talk about when three of the sentences in Activity 1 described your life.

When I went to the mountains with my grandpa, I exercised for so long that my legs ached.

When I went swimming last Monday, I swam for such a long time that my arms ached.

Mission Stage 2

Make a list of tips for feeling better. Share your list with your friend. Do they have any good ideas you missed?

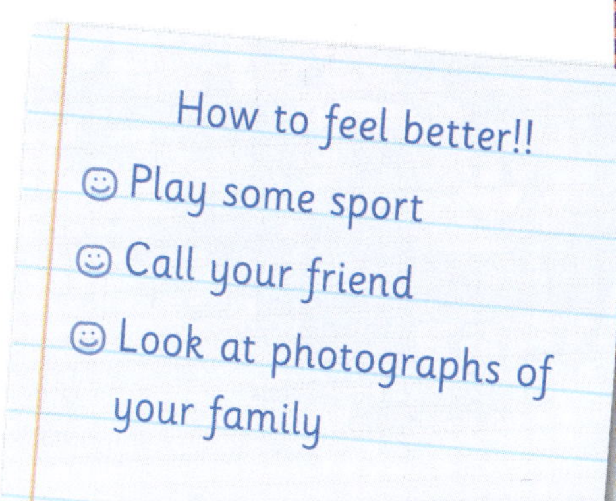

1 In pairs, talk about the questions.

1 What does a cowboy do?

2 Where do wolves live? What do they eat?

3.07 The cowboy who cried wolf

Life on the ranch was quiet. Everyone worked hard to grow plants and look after the animals, and they fell asleep straight away when night came. But one night, a noise woke them all up. AHR-WOOOOO! They knew that noise! It was a wolf, and there were a lot of calves on the ranch. Somebody would need to make sure that no wolves got into the fields.

Buck was the youngest cowboy on the ranch and he was always looking for excitement. Early the next morning Cody, one of the older cowboys, said to Buck, 'You have to stay here today and look after the calves. There are wolves about! If you see one you should shout, "Wolf!" The people on the ranch will come and help you.' Buck was annoyed. He wanted to ride with the others! But he had to do what Cody said. So, the cowboys rode off to the west and Buck stayed in the field to look after the calves.

Buck was so bored! He had no one to talk to, and no wolves came. Buck stared so hard that his eyes hurt. Hours passed and Buck was miserable. Finally, he had an idea. 'The ranch workers will come and talk to me if a wolf comes,' he thought. He jumped up and shouted, 'Wolf!' At once men came running from the ranch. His little sister, Blossom, came too.

'Where's the wolf?' shouted the men. 'It was over there,' said Buck. 'But it went away when I shouted.' The men waited for a few minutes, but when they didn't see a wolf, they went back to their work.

'Did you really see a wolf?' Blossom asked Buck. 'Of course, I did,' he said. Blossom gave him a strange look. Buck felt embarrassed, but Blossom didn't say anything.

The next day Buck wanted to go with the other cowboys, but Cody was worried about wolves. 'You must stay and look after the calves again,' he said. So, Buck stayed! Day after day, it was the same thing, looking at a dull field of cows. By the fourth day, he was so bored and lonely that he shouted, 'Wolf!' again. Once more the men from the ranch ran to help him. They were amazed when they didn't see a wolf attacking the calves. 'Where's the wolf?' they called to Buck. 'It was over there,' said Buck. 'But it ran away when I shouted.' 'Are you sure you saw a wolf?' asked a man called Jeb. 'I definitely saw one!' said Buck. 'That's why I shouted.' The men from the ranch went away again, complaining.

Blossom was furious with her brother. 'There was NO wolf,' she said to Buck. 'You mustn't shout "wolf" again. Everybody is very annoyed with you!'

The next day Buck suddenly heard AHR-WOOOOOO! He jumped up. It wasn't one wolf! It was 3 … 4 … 5 … a pack of wolves! 'Wolves! Wolves! Wolves!' screamed Buck. But nobody came. They didn't believe him anymore! Buck ran at the wolves, shouting. But it was too late. All the calves were dead and Buck knew he would be in BIG trouble …

2 In pairs, talk about the questions.

1 Who or what is responsible for the death of the calves? Why?
2 Do you ever tell lies? Why?/Why not? When might you tell a lie?
3 How do you think Buck feels when he realises he's made a mistake? Do you think he feels bad for telling lies?

1 **Look at the pictures below.** What different emotions can you see?

2 3.08 **Listen and read the text.** Why is it good to understand how other people feel?

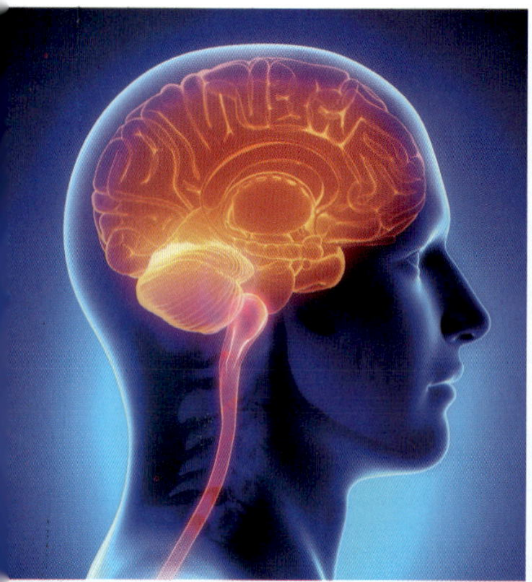

Emotional awareness

We can feel different things on different days. Sometimes we feel miserable because we had an argument with a friend and sometimes we feel worried about something. It's important to understand our feelings and learn how to show them so that we don't make our friends, our family and ourselves sad.

Babies and children show their emotions by laughing or crying because they can't say what they feel and why. As we grow up, we learn how to understand how we are feeling. This is called emotional awareness. It also helps us have good relationships with other people.

When we feel strong emotions or we are stressed there are chemicals in our brains that can make us feel happy, annoyed or sad. This chemical is called cortisol. It can be good for us because it gives us energy. However, if we feel too stressed then we have too much cortisol in our brains and it's difficult to sleep.

When you see your friends, you might be able to work out what they are feeling by their faces. How do you think these people feel?

It's good to think about how other people are feeling too. For example, if your friend is sad that he didn't get onto the football team and you are sad with him, you are sharing his sadness – this is called empathy. Have you ever seen that your dad is annoyed when he has to tidy your things? If you think about how your dad feels and understand that he's doing extra work and why he might feel annoyed … that's also empathy.

Empathy and emotional awareness are important for all relationships – at home, at school and at work when we are older. It helps you to understand more about the people and the world around you.

3 **Read the text again and say *yes* or *no*.**

1 We need to understand our own feelings before we can understand other peoples'.

2 Cortisol helps us sleep.

3 We can sometimes understand how friends feel by looking at them.

4 Adults often feel empathy when they have to tidy things.

5 You should think about how other people feel in all situations.

4 **In pairs, talk about things you can do when you are feeling stressed or sad.**

When I feel stressed, I like to go outside for a walk.

I like playing my guitar.

1 Look at the title and the picture and answer the questions.

1 Why do you think the club in this text is so amazing?

2 What could the boy's dream be?

2 Read the text and check your ideas.

1 An amazing club!!

2 Ben Bampton's just started a school club called 'Helping Dreams'. He became interested after reading about a company that helps schoolchildren who feel bored or worried. I told my dad, 'I'd like to do something like that too.' 'Let's call that company now!' he answered. 'That's how I learned about finding pieces of machines or clothes and inventing something new with them. I sell the new objects during the lunch break. The money I get helps kids in our area who feel alone. I now understand that if you want to help people, you should do it as a team.'

3 'You don't need to know lots of facts or be good at science in my club. You can make a new game from an old CD player or some jewellery from used handbags.'

4 Ben's simple idea has grown and his town thinks his club is fantastic! Ben would like to start his own business soon. He's finding ways to make his helpful ideas cost less. He plans to have 'Helping Dreams' clubs in every school, so any child who wants to build something can join the team for free.

5 Ben feels amazed because his club is so popular and says, 'It's important to talk to someone when you feel unhappy at school. You should try to have fun with friends, and my club helps with that, too! Anything is possible! Look at me and my dream!'

3 Read the text again. Match the ideas (A–E) to the title and paragraphs (1–5).

A This tells me what the text is about. 1

B A boy's interest in starting a club. ___

C The boy's future plans. ___

D The boy's advice. ___

E What you can do in the club. ___

4 Where does the writer or Ben say this? Find the sentences in the text.

- The money helps other children who live near the school.
- You don't need to get good marks if you want to be in the club.
- The boy's next project is to have his own business.
- Share your problems at school with someone.

5 Read the question and choose the correct answer.

Ben plans to …

A be more popular.

B have clubs like his in more schools.

C be healthier at school.

EXAM TIP! Practise reading texts **quickly** for **main ideas** and then **more carefully** to find **details**.

1 **In groups, talk about what you do to relax before a school exam or test.**

> I go to my friend's house.

> I eat a snack with my sister. She's so funny!

> I read my favourite book.

2 **Read the start of the conversation and complete the instructions.**

You will hear (1) __________ talking to her friend (2) __________ about (3) __________ .

Sophie Hi Yuri, what's the matter? Have you got a cold?

Yuri I'm very tired actually. I'm not sleeping enough at the moment.

Sophie Are you worried about your science test?

Yuri Yes, I had a maths test yesterday and history today. If I don't sleep well, I won't get a good mark …

3 3.09 **Listen and check. What advice could you give to Yuri?**

4 **Look at the example answer. Why is A the best answer?**

Example: 0 What's wrong with Yuri at the moment?

(**A**) He's tired. **B** He's got a temperature. **C** He's got a cold.

5 **What are the questions about? Put them in the right group.**

Who feels tired at the moment? Which test did Yuri do yesterday?
What does Yuri do to stop feeling worried? Which two things shouldn't he use late at night?
Who believes that good sleep helps memory? Who feels better now?

Facts	Opinions	Feelings
		Who feels tired at the moment?

6 3.10 **Listen to the conversation. Answer the questions from Activity 5.**

EXAM TIP! Before you listen, look at the questions. Do they ask you for a fact, opinion or feeling? Think of phrases we use for these things. For example:
In fact … **I'm sure …** **I'm worried …**

1 Look at the signs and choose the correct words to complete the sentences.

1 

You **needn't** / **must** worry. It's OK to drink this water.

2 

You **don't have to** / **shouldn't** swim here. It's dangerous!

3 

You **should** / **mustn't** walk here. You oughtn't to run.

4 

You **have to** / **mustn't** touch this sign. You might cut yourself.

5 

You **must** / **needn't** turn off your phone here. People are studying.

6 

You **shouldn't** / **have to** put food in this bin. It's only for paper.

2 Write one sentence using *so … that* or *such … that*.

1 I felt bored during the film. I fell asleep.
I felt so bored during the film that I fell asleep.

2 I think it's a fun gym. I go after school every day.

3 She does exercise carefully. She never gets injured.

4 I think painting is fun. I tell all my friends to try it.

5 I had a bad headache. I couldn't stand up.

6 I played football for a long time. I had to lie down to recover.

3 Choose ten words from this unit. Record the words using the steps below.

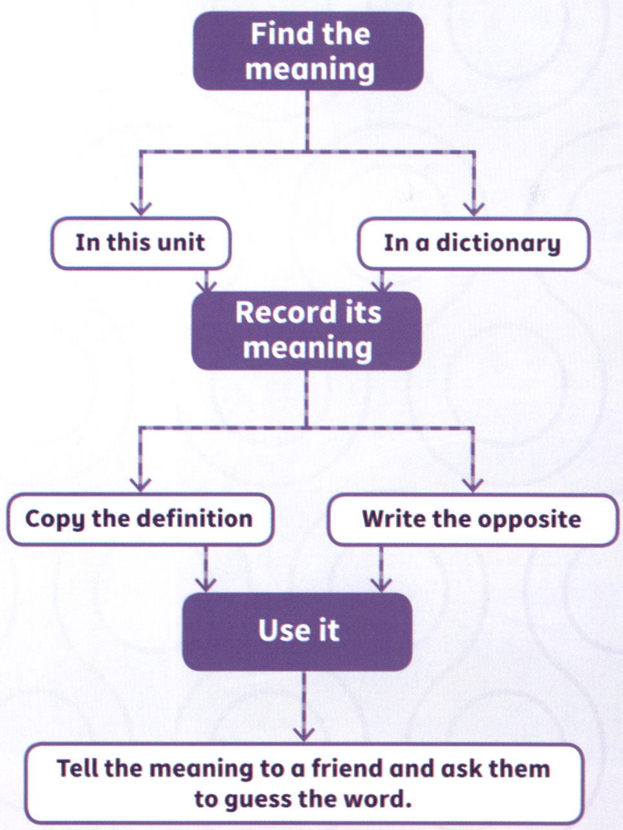

Mission in action!

Make a feelings wheel with real suggestions.

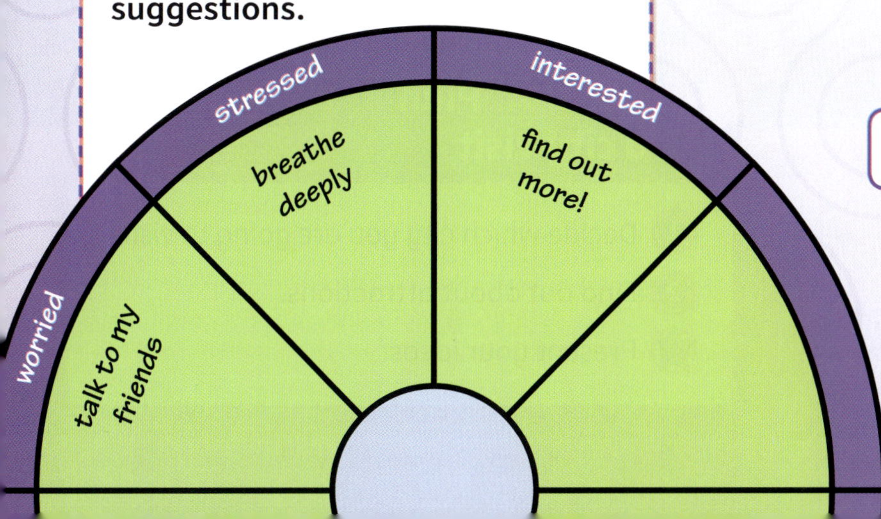

8 Pretty cities

1

2

3

4

5

6

7

8

9

What can you see in each picture? Which place would you like to visit most? Why?

Watch the video. What do Jim and Jenny say is the best thing to do in London?

Mission Plan a city visit

1. Decide which city you are going to visit.
2. Find out about attractions.
★ Present your ideas.

1 3.11 **Look at the adverts for city tours.** Match the pictures (1–10) to the words in bold in the advert. Then listen and check.

Boat tour of Toronto

Only $19!!

- See the city from the water on our one-hour **cruise**.
- Learn about Toronto's history and **monuments**.
- Take photos of some of Canada's most famous buildings and **towers**.

1

2

3

Art tour of New York

- Visit a **gallery** and see one of the U.S.A.'s best art collections.
- See amazing **sculptures** as we walk through New York's streets.
- The tour ends at a music **festival** in a park – so bring your dance shoes!

4

5

6

London sports tour

Call 020 7946 0949 for more information

- Take a **sightseeing** bus tour of London's most famous sports stadiums.
- Look round the Wimbledon Lawn Tennis museum and it's amazing **collection** of tennis prizes.
- The tour goes past Buckingham **Palace** and finishes at London's famous sports **department store**.

7

8

9

10

2 **Write sentences about which places your class would like to visit.**

We'd love ____________

____

We wouldn't mind

____

____

We wouldn't like

____

____

3 **A teacher is going to take some students on one of the tours. In pairs, talk about the tours and say which the students would find most interesting.**

I think her class would love to visit a gallery and look at the sculptures.

Me too! And I think they wouldn't mind going on a river cruise because they could take lots of amazing photos.

EXAM TIP! To give opinions, say what would or wouldn't be a good option and **why**.

1 **Look at the pictures and choose the correct words to complete the sentences.**

1 I think the building is probably in **London** / **New York** / **Toronto**.

2 I think the building is probably a **department store** / **monument** / **gallery**.

3 I think the painting might be by **Da Vinci** / **Van Gogh** / **Monet**.

2 3.12 **Listen to a radio show called Charlies' Challenge and check your answers to Activity 1.**

3 3.13 **Listen again, and write the correct answers.**

Charlies' Challenge

About

The gallery has around **(1)** ________ paintings.

Tickets are: **(2)** ________ for children

Has amazing pictures like Van Gogh's **(3)** *The* ________ *Night*

Information

Website: **(4)** www.________.org

Phone number: **(5)** ________

EXAM TIP!
Make sure you **read the notes and question** before the recording starts. Can you think of any possible answers before you listen?

4 **In pairs, answer the questions.**

1 Is there a gallery like this where you live?

2 Would you like to go on a school trip to this gallery?

Grammar look: indirect questions

'How many paintings are there?'

'Do you know how many paintings there are?'

1 Indirect questions are usually **more** / **less** polite then normal questions.

2 When we use indirect questions, the word order **changes** / **stays the same**.

page 126

1 3.14 **PRONUNCIATION Listen and repeat.** page 119

2 Put the words in order to make questions.

1 what I can see / please? / Could you tell me / at the museum,

____

2 what / Do you know / time / closes? / the museum

____

3 the museum / where / please? / Could you tell me / is,

____

4 how / tickets / please? / much / Could you tell me / are

____

5 the / please? / Could you tell me / museum's / phone number,

____

6 if / Do you know / take photos / I can / at the museum?

____

3 Answer the questions from Activity 2 about one of the museums below.

Tickets:
Adults, $14,
Children (aged 5–17), $5

What you can see:
Old shoes, famous people's shoes and much more!

Opening times: 10 am–5 pm
(10 am–8 pm on Thursdays)

Finding us:
We're on 327 Bloor Street West, in Toronto

Call us on: 0523 6498 213

Photos: You can take photos anywhere in the museum.

LONDON TRANSPORT MUSEUM

Tickets:
Adult £17.50;
Free for children (under 18)

You can see:
Old buses, trains, taxis and many other things

Opening hours:
10:00 am–6:00 pm
on Monday – Thursday, Saturday and Sunday
Fridays 10:00 am–8:00 pm

Address:
Covent Garden Piazza, near the River Thames

Phone number:
0625 9587 31

Bring a camera because you can take photos in the museum!

Mission Stage 1

Decide which city you are going to visit.

1 **Read Jim's blog.** Do you think these places are boring or beautiful?

Jim's Big Blog

Last week, Jenny and I visited London. While Jenny took photos of the famous places in London, I took photos of things that might look boring – but that I think are amazing.

Boring or beautiful? My photos of London

Jenny said, 'Oh Jim! You're not taking a photo of that, are you?'

Some people say that this is London's most beautiful roundabout! That's because of the amazing glass building in the middle of the **roundabout**. In the building is a **booking office** where you can buy tickets and a cinema with the largest screen in Britain!

Jenny said, 'That's just a car park, Jim!'

This **car park** was built in 1928 – and, with 1,000 spaces, it used to be the biggest car park in the country! It used to have two different restaurants inside, too. When it was built, there was even a plan to put a golf course on the top of it. Today, the building's still a car park but sometimes events like fashion or film shows happen there.

Jenny said, 'This is the ugliest place we've been all day!'

I think this station's amazing. It opened in 1863 – that's more than 150 years ago! In fact, London had the first **underground** stations in the world. Today the trains are electric, but they didn't use to be. They used to make the air very dirty!

Jenny said, 'Really Jim? ANOTHER photo?!'

This **signpost** made me laugh a lot. It was on a normal **pavement** in London! There are lots of interesting street names in London, like Brick Lane and Pie Corner. Can you guess what used to be made on those streets?

Jenny said, 'Can't we get a map and go?'

This is the **tourist information** centre in London. Jenny went there to get a map and find out the **opening hours** for a gallery. While Jenny was chatting and Mum was getting some money from a **cash machine**, I took this photo. I love this building because it's very new, but looks amazing next to the old buildings nearby. The building is also good for the environment – its roof collects water to use in its toilets and for its gardens.

2 **Match the definitions (A–I) to the words in bold in Jim's blog.**

A Something that you walk on, next to a road
B Somewhere that you get money
C The times that a place is open
D Somewhere people leave cars
E Something next to a road that gives you information
F A train that travels under the streets
G Somewhere where you can buy tickets
H Somewhere you can ask questions about a new city
I Somewhere roads meet and that cars drive around

3 **Look at the pictures in Jim's blog.** Which words in bold in the blog can you see? Which words can't you see?

Grammar look: *used to / didn't use to*

'They used to make the air very dirty.'

'Today the trains are electric, but they didn't use to be.'

'Can you guess what used to be made on those streets?'

1 Did trains make the air dirty in the past? **Yes / No**

2 How many times did this happen? **Often / Only once**

3 Does it happen now? **Yes / No**

Used to means that things happened **(4) often / once** in the past. They **(5) still / don't** happen now. It's also used for facts that were true, but aren't now.

page 126

1 **Guess which of the facts (1–4) is false.**

Hey Sally, I've just visited William Shakespeare's Theatre in London! Three of these facts about Shakespeare are true. Can you guess which one is false?

1 Shakespeare used to live in London.

2 Women didn't use to act in Shakespeare's plays.

3 Shakespeare used to like watching football.

4 Shakespeare's brother Edmund Shakespeare also used to write plays.

2 **Write three true sentences and one false sentence about yourself.** Use *used to* or *didn't use to*. In groups, guess the false sentences.

Mission Stage 2

Find out more about the attractions in the city.

Search

All Maps Images Settings Tools

About 1,200 results (0.36 seconds)

You can see the whole of the city from the top of the fairground!

Literature

1 **What can you see in the pictures?** What do you think the novel is about?

3.16

Chapter One
The case of the Butterfly Diamond

He got the message at midnight. 'Bad news. Arabella Von Thursday's stolen The Butterfly Diamond. Can you help?' Of course he could help! He was Johnny Ming after all, and helping was what he did. From Monday to Friday he was a successful businessman, the manager of Ming's Marvels, a three-storey furniture shop in Old Shanghai. But at the weekend, he did something a little different – and what could be more different than being 'China's Number 1 Secret Detective'?

'We think she's going to sell it somewhere in England,' said Huxley on the phone. 'Do you know when the exhibition starts?' asked Johnny Ming. 'Next Tuesday,' said Huxley, sounding worried. 'You must get here right away!' Yes, thought Johnny Ming as he packed his suitcase. I must get there right away, and you must reduce your stress. Huxley used to be a relaxed and happy man, but there was so much to worry about these days, especially Countess Arabella Von Thursday. She was a dangerous criminal who stole paintings, sculptures and now diamonds. If she wasn't stopped, the great museums of the world would soon be empty.

In the full-length mirror next to the front door, Johnny Ming looked at himself one more time. His white suit was perfectly clean and his black tie was just right. The brown and white leather shoes he was wearing were so shiny that you could see your face in them. He checked the time on his pocket watch, then tied it to his belt by a chain. Before locking his suitcase, he checked that he had everything – red and white toothbrush, clothes for various climates, a wooden tennis racket, a big box of milk chocolates and enough apple juice for seventy-two hours. He pushed up his Panama hat and tapped his walking stick on the floorboard. He was ready to go. Blowing out the long line of candles in the hall, he said to the dark, 'You won't win this time, Arabella Von Thursday!'

Minutes later Johnny Ming was flying above the rubbish and traffic jams of the city. He smiled to himself. Alone in Blue Wonder, his beloved hot-air balloon, he had time to ... what was that? Something was moving near his feet.

Looking down, he saw two pairs of eyes. 'Stand up immediately!' he said. The girls were no more than eleven years old. Johnny Ming breathed in deeply. China's Number One Secret Detective mustn't be too annoyed. 'What is the meaning of this?' he asked as calmly as he could. 'I'm Mia,' said the one with the black hair. 'And I'm Sami,' said the one with the red hair. 'And we know where the Butterfly Diamond is,' they said together. Johnny Ming's mouth was open, but he couldn't speak. 'If you let us help you,' said Sami. 'We won't tell anyone who you really are.' 'Well,' said Mia as she crossed her arms. 'What do you say, Mr Ming?'

2 **In pairs, role play a conversation.** Imagine you are Sami and Mia waiting in the hot-air balloon for Johnny Ming.

STUDENT A You are Sami. You are worried. You think you and Mia have done the wrong thing. You think Johnny Ming will be angry with you.

STUDENT B You are Mia. You aren't worried. You think you and Sami have done the right thing. You think Johnny Ming will be excited to have two helpers.

But we don't know where the Butterfly Diamond is, Mia! What will Johnny Ming say when we tell him?

It's OK, Sami. If we help Johnny Ming, we'll become secret detectives like him!

Cross-curricular

1 **Look at the pictures and match them to the headings (1–4).**

1 Don't feed the animals ☐
2 Respect local customs and traditions ☐
3 Protect the environment ☐
4 Support local communities ☐

A

B

C

D

2 3.17 **Listen and read the text.** What ideas from Activity 1 are good for Uluru?

When you visit another country, do you think about where you put your rubbish? Do you look at the signposts and do what they say? Do you learn about the people that live there and do the same things that they do? If the answer is yes to these questions, then you are an ecotourist!

A good example of ecotourism is in Australia. This is Uluru (Ayers Rock) in Australia. Lots of tourists used to visit the rock and climb it. But they were damaging it and they weren't respecting local customs. Uluru used to belong to the Aboriginal people of Australia and they didn't use to climb it because it was an important place for them. So, in 1985 the Australian government gave it back to the Aboriginal people and now most tourists don't climb it.

There are national parks all around the world. They cover about 6% of the Earth's surface.

3 3.18 **Listen and write the correct answers.**

Timanfaya National Park

Location: Lanzarote, the Canary Islands, Spain
Size: (1) ___________
Popular name of the park:
(2) ___________
Transport: (3) ___________
Interesting activity: (4) ___________
Type of food: (5) ___________

4 **Choose a holiday location in your country.** Make a list of ways that people can be responsible tourists there.

1 **Read and write the words in a sentence.** What are the different meanings?

travel trip tour

2 **Read the text below.** Can you guess the words you don't know?

A modern travel company

Cities **(1)** _____ important places and our company, City Tourism, **(2)** _____ to help visitors explore and have fun.

Choose a **(3)** _____ with us and you'll be really surprised at how many different activities there are. The people you stay **(4)** _____ teach you something new and then you go sightseeing. For example, learn about garden bees or make bright costumes for a festival. Afterwards, you can go on a tour of the colourful street art. It's our most popular activity, so book early!

Many **(5)** _____ come back every year. This year we are going to build little houses to look **(6)** _____ the animals that live in the city. We will keep you **(7)** _____ so it doesn't matter how old you are, you'll never be bored!

3 **Read the text again.** For each question, choose the correct answer. **Why are the other choices incorrect?**

	A		B		C	
2	A	wants	B	can	C	need
3	A	holiday	B	journey	C	trips
4	A	by	B	with	C	at
5	A	passengers	B	families	C	visitor
6	A	after	B	for	C	to
7	A	noisy	B	tired	C	busy

Example:

1 **A** is **B** isn't **C** are

Answer: **A** **B** **C**

EXAM TIP! **Practise reading** all kinds of short texts and guess words you don't know.

1 In pairs, talk about the types of holidays you enjoy.

I like going to visit my family at the beach, because it's sunny. What about you?

I prefer to go to the city. My brother and I love shopping!

2 Look at the title. Read the text quickly. What is the text about?

Our unusual holidays

We **(1)** used to have boring, sightseeing holidays. My dad always wanted to go to museums! But **(2)** ________ days my family and I travel around the world visiting strange places. Before, we used to stay in hotels, but now we normally go camping.

We decided to go to the mountains because I love **(3)** ________ photos of wild animals with my digital camera. The **(4)** ________ exciting thing is where we sleep – our tent is high on the side of the mountain! I love it, but my sister feels **(5)** ________ worried that she can't sleep.

There are lots of animals there, and it can be dangerous. If you decide to go, you **(6)** ________ hide your food so a bear doesn't look for some in your tent!

3 Read the text above. Look at the first answer. Why is it correct?

4 Look at the text below. What kinds of words are missing?

On the river in Copenhagen

I think the best way **(1)** ________ visitors to see Copenhagen is by going on a different kind of river cruise. It's not very expensive and it's even a good way to **(2)** ________ some exercise!

In December, lots of people go to the river and take a kayak to celebrate the end of **(3)** ________ year. There are lots of lights **(4)** ________ it gets very dark in the winter! Everyone starts singing and then they travel along the river. You can pass by the parks and gardens, as well **(5)** ________ the most famous monuments.

The city looks beautiful but it can get very cold, so make sure you bring a big coat! **(6)** ________ favourite part is having a delicious hot chocolate with my family afterwards.

5 Read and write the correct answer.

EXAM TIP! Remember to think about the **type of word** you need in the space.

1 Choose the correct indirect questions.

1 A Do you know where Buckingham Palace is?
  B Do you know where is Buckingham Palace?

2 A Could you tell me what time does the cinema open, please?
  B Could you tell me what time the cinema opens, please?

3 A Do you remember how much were the cruise tickets?
  B Do you remember how much the cruise tickets were?

4 A Would you mind explaining how I can get to the National Gallery?
  B Would you mind explaining how can I get to the National Gallery?

5 A Do you know who is that?
  B Do you know who that is?

6 A Could you explain why the building is good for the environment, please?
  B Could you explain why is the building good for the environment, please?

2 Complete the sentences with *used to* and a verb.

1 Five years ago, I __________ on the underground a lot, but now I usually travel by bus.

2 I __________ a stamp collection. But I gave it to my friend last year.

3 I __________ in London. But I moved last year and now I live in a small village.

4 I usually go shopping at a department store. But I __________ shopping at the market.

5 The building in the town centre __________ a palace, but now it's a gallery.

6 The tourist information centre __________ at 9:30. But these days it opens at 11:00.

3 Choose ten words from this unit. Record the words using the steps below.

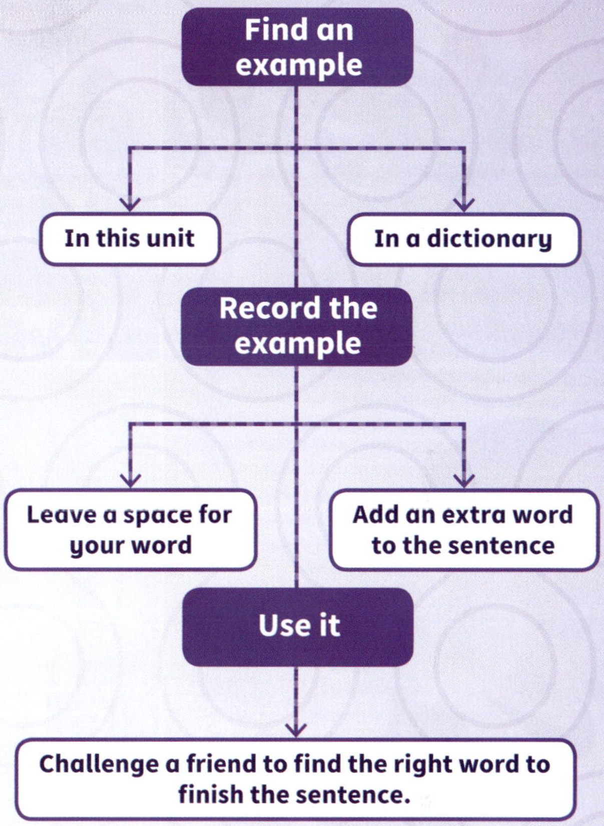

Mission in action!

Present ideas about the city you chose and what you can do there.

9 Lights, camera, action!

1

2

3

4

5

6

7

8

9

Mission Make a scene for a film or TV show

1. Make a mind map.
2. Plan a storyboard.
3. ★ Present your scene. Choose the best ones!

What do the the pictures have to do with entertainment? Which things are familiar to you?

Watch the video. Why does the lemon hate Jenny?

1 **Look at the TV guide.** Match the words in the box to the pictures (1–9).

the news	a cartoon	a chat show	a comedy	a drama
a horror film	a documentary	an action film	a quiz show	

What's picture number 1?

It's an action film.

This week on TV …

Popular now | Recommended for you | Watch it again

1

Evil men have taken Doug's dog – but he'll do anything to get it back.

2
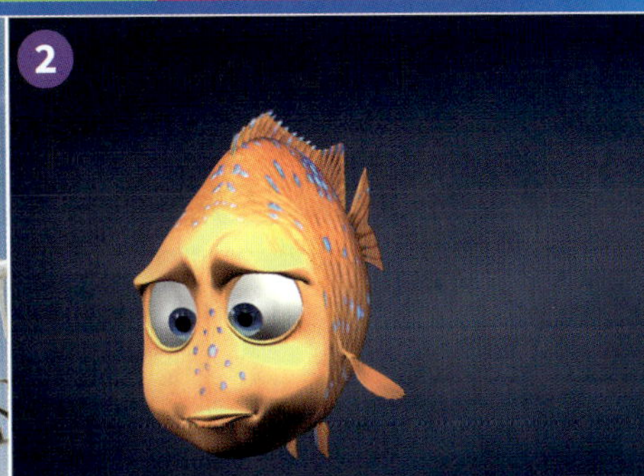
Nemo is lost and his dad goes on a long journey to find him.

3

Interviews with top stars.

4

Join us for more lunchtime laughs!

5

Learn about the life of turtles near the beaches of Mexico.

6

Clara tells Tony the truth about the broken table.

7

The latest stories from around the world.

8

Lost. Scared. Alone. And there's something terrible in the forest …

9

We ask families what they know. Let's find out!

2 3.19 **Listen and check.**

3 3.20 **PRONUNCIATION** **Listen and repeat.** page 119

PHOTOS BLOG LINKS CHATS

A

Question from:

Eiffel_64

Hey guys,

You're all coming to my birthday party next weekend, aren't you? I'm really excited about it. Mum's having a special superhero cake made for me and we're going to watch a film. But I want to ask you something. Can you all dress up as your favourite film character? I think that would be so cool! I'm going to dress up as Batman, of course.

B

CatGirl_22

Hey Eiffel_64. Cool! I'd LOVE to dress up as my favourite film character. Can you guess who it is? Spiderman, of course! I think Spiderman's cooler than Batman because he's part spider and part man. My dad has had a spider costume made for me so I'll wear that.

C

FriendlyJ

Hey, that's such a great idea! My favourite film is *Finding Nemo*. Have you seen it? It's a cartoon and a comedy about a fish called Nemo and his dad. One day Nemo gets caught by a boat and is sent to live in a dentist's office. I'd like to dress as Nemo but I don't have time to make a fish costume. So I think I'll come as a clown instead because Nemo's a clown fish! Do you think that's OK? I could have my face painted too!

D

Sharky_McMarky

Can I dress up as a penguin? My favourite film is a documentary called *March of the Penguins* – you should watch it. I love it so much that last year I had penguin-shaped ice creams made for my birthday. Did you know that father penguins look after the eggs while the mothers are looking for food? When the eggs become baby penguins, they have to wait a long time for their mothers to feed them. Will there be lots of food at your party?

1 **Read the posts quickly.** Who will each child dress as? Match the posts (A–D) to pictures (1–4).

1
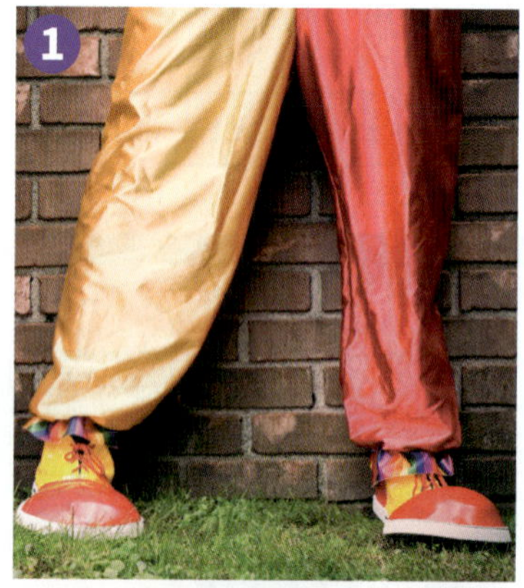

2

3

4

2 **Read Eiffel_64's post again.** Say *yes* or *no*.

1 Eiffel_64's birthday party is next Monday. — No!

2 Eiffel_64 will watch a film at the party.

3 Eiffel_64 thinks his friends should all wear suits to the party.

4 Batman is Eiffel_64's favourite film character.

3 **Write two yes/no sentences about one of the posts.** In pairs, say your sentences.

Catgirl_22 wants to dress up as Batman.

No, she wants to dress up as Spiderman.

Grammar look: causative *have/get*

'Mum's having a special superhero cake made for me.'

1 Will Eiffel_64's mum make the cake herself? **Yes / No**

2 Who will make the cake? **someone at a cake shop / the boy**

3 We use *have* when we have asked someone to do something for us. We **do / don't** do it ourselves. In informal situations, we can use *get* instead of *have*.

page 126

1 3.22 **Read and match the script ideas (1–4) to A–D.** Listen and check.

1 Sarah moves to a dark, old house a long way from the town. One day she …

2 A grey goat lives on a mountain and feels very lonely. But one day, he gets …

3 A farmer lives in a quiet village in a little old spaceship. One day he has his …

4 Two brothers were organising a birthday party. They had …

A his hair dyed pink. Lots of people start visiting the mountain to see him and take his photo. He's the most famous animal on the hill …

B a cool cake made, their faces painted and lots of pizzas delivered. But when the party started, there was one problem they hadn't thought of …

C has the walls repainted in a beautiful green. But when she goes to eat breakfast the next morning, the colour of the paint is different.

D lights fixed by a strange old woman. 'Your lights turn on and off now, but don't press that big red button,' she warns.

2 **Choose one script idea from Activity 1 and finish it.**

At first, the goat loves seeing so many people. But the cars coming to see him are noisy, and some people leave litter on the hill.

Mission Stage 1

Make a mind map for a three minute scene.

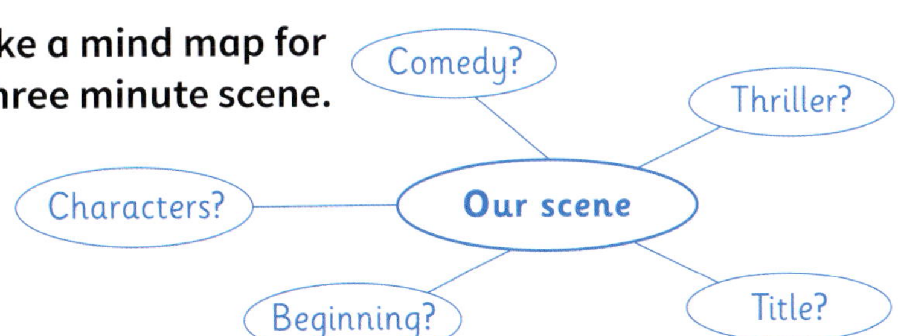

1 3.23 **Look at the pictures.** Listen to Mark's podcast. Which idea is not in the pictures?

2 3.24 **Listen again.** Put the pictures in the order that you hear them.

A 
travelling to China to film

B 
paying famous actors

C 
building old rooms in a studio

D 
making advertisements for the film

E 
spending money on special effects

F 
buying dance shoes

3 3.25 **Complete the sentences from Mark's podcast.** Use the words in the box. Listen and check.

adverts	celebrity	channel	heroine/hero	interviewing	performance	programmes	review	series	scene	studio

1 I'm ________ my classmates to ask what they would do if they had $250 million to make a film.
2 I'd love to work with a famous actor. Someone who's a big ________ .
3 The ________ is the most important person in most films.
4 I'd spend the money by building lots of old rooms in a ________ .
5 I'd spend the money on ________ . It's really important that everyone knows about new films.
6 I'd love to make a TV ________ about tigers. I'd make six ________ that are each 30 minutes long.
7 That'd be great for the nature ________ .
8 So I'd have one ________ with the heroine flying above a city.
9 We're doing a dance ________ at the theatre next week.
10 Maybe Jenny can ________ it for her blog?

Grammar look: the second conditional

'If I had $250 million, I'd buy cameras and costumes for the actors.'

'If there was someone well-known in my film, I think it'd be really popular.'

1 Is having $250 million to make a film possible? **Yes / No**

2 Is it likely? **Yes / No**

3 Will there be someone well known in the film? **Probably / Probably not**

4 Will the film be popular? **Probably / Probably not**

5 We use the second conditional to talk about something that is **likely / not likely** to happen.

page 127

1 Complete the email with the words in the box. Write one word in each gap.

had what would if ~~was~~

EXAM TIP! Look at the words that come **before and after** the gap.

Dear Claire,

I (1) was watching TV yesterday, when I decided I'd like to make a film. It'd be a documentary about our town. (2) ______ I was allowed, I'd film at the zoo. I love the animals there! If I (3) ______ a lot of money, I'd get a celebrity to be in the film. What about you? (4) ______ would you do if you had money to make a film? If you could ask any celebrity, who (5) ______ be in your film?

See you soon!

Simon

2 What would you do if you had $250 million to make a film? Write four ideas. Share your ideas. Which idea do you like best?

If I had $250 million, I'd make my film in space.

3 Tell a chain story.

If Tim had a million dollars, he'd buy a big house.

If Tim had a big house, he'd keep lots of camels there.

If Tim kept lots of camels, they'd eat all the flowers in his garden.

Mission Stage 2

In groups, make a storyboard for your scene.

If I had more money, I'd run away.

1 **Read the title and look at the pictures.** What do you think the monster is?

The Monster in our Homes

3.26

I think you're probably not aware
Of the terrible monster sitting there.
Inside your house, right under your nose,
'Cos everyone's got one, but nobody knows.

It's big and ugly and usually black,
It waits and waits, ready to attack.
When you sit down and switch it on,
You can't escape it and then you're gone.

The screen catches you and you sit and stare,
You really don't know how long you're there.
Your eyes get tired and sleepy and red,
And Mum keeps shouting, 'It's time for bed!'

Children are one of its favourite things,
It shows them heroes and monsters with wings.
Cartoons and quiz shows, movies and more,
Means that kids can't move from their place on the floor.

And even though it seems free and fun,
If I were you I'd get out and run.
Because there's no doubt, it can change your mind,
With the silly ideas that you might find.

Parents often say, 'Your eyes will go square.'
And some kids respond, 'I think that's unfair!'
But take the remote and they'll shout and scream,
And others I've heard can get really mean!

But there is a solution against this terrible enemy,
Just think about kids in the past generally.
They had no technology, not even a phone,
But had lots of friends and were never alone.

They played in the streets with their friends, they were happy,
They skipped, rode bikes and were very chatty.
Some rode to the library and even took out a book,
They got lost in adventures with Captain Cook.

So if you've got a house with a monster within,
I'd get rid of it now, I'd throw it straight in the bin.
I'd think twice about watching so much television,
I'd find other things to do and I'd make that my mission!

2 In pairs, talk about the questions.

1 Does the poet think the monster is good or bad? Why?
2 Why isn't it a good idea to watch too much TV?
3 How much TV do you watch?
4 What do you like to watch on TV?

1 **Look at the pictures.** How do you think they are relevant to films?

2 3.27 **Listen and read the text.** How were special effects different in the past?

Special effects in film

Have you ever watched a film and thought, 'How did the hero fly?' or 'How did they film that action on a burning ship?' Film makers make these scenes by using special effects. These are artificial images that look like they are real but are created by artists and technical experts.

Quite often the action is filmed on a green screen and then special effects are added on a computer. Sometimes the effects are so good that the experts win awards for their work.

Special effects in the past

Before the use of CGI (computer generated images) in cinema, it was difficult to make exciting special effects that looked real. Special effects artists used optical illusions and visual effects like painted sets, complicated make-up or models.

The Great and Powerful Oz has lots of amazing special effects, but there is an older version of the film called *The Wizard of Oz* which was made in 1939. There is a famous scene when a tornado (a dangerous wind storm) hits a farm in Kansas, USA. The film makers created the tornado by using a very long sock made of thin material which they filled with sand. Then they blew it round and round with a powerful electric fan! There are lots of other basic special effects in the film which at the time were very exciting.

Make your own special effects

You can make your own special effects using your mobile phone or objects at home. Try putting a pencil into a clear glass full of water and then look at the pencil through the glass – how does it look? There are lots of apps that you can use which put special effects on photos – you can be an animal or take photos and change the way they look. We can even have videos changed on our phones – why not try it?

3 **Read the text again and answer the questions.**

1 What does CGI mean?
2 When was *The Wizard of Oz* made?
3 How did they make the tornado?
4 What effects can we use on our phones?

4 **You are a film maker and you haven't got a computer.** In pairs, talk about how to make the scenes below.

- a landing on the moon
- a trip under the sea
- a snow storm

1 **Look and read.** Do you need all of these things to tell a story? Which do you think is the most important?

characters action a place a time names

2 **Look at picture A and answer the questions.**

A

1 Who are the characters? What are their names?
____

2 Where are they? _______________

3 What are they doing? _______________

3 **Read the beginning of the story.** What things in picture A does this student write about?

Last night, Oliver and his brother went to the cinema.
Oliver bought some snacks while Peter bought the tickets.

4 **Look at picture B and read the middle of the story.** Which type of film does the student write about?

... the tickets. They sat down and the monster film started.

B

5 **Look at picture C. What happened?** Tell your partner. Use the words in the box or your own words.

a brave hero special effects was scared
funny laughed pointed

C

6 **Write about the end of the story.**

Peter was scared!

____

____

7 **Swap stories.** Give your friend's story a mark. 1 is poor and 5 is excellent. Write three things they can do to improve.

EXAM TIP! Try to write between 35 and 45 words. You will **lose marks** if you write less than 35 words.

1 **Read the question and Katerina's reply. What has Tanya forgotten to include in her email?** ________________

You must answer this question. Write your answer in about 100 words.
Read this message from your English-speaking friend Tanya and the notes you have made.

TO:
FROM: Tanya

Hello!

What programmes or films have you watched on TV this week? — **Describe the best one.**

I saw the first episode of the new celebrity chat show on Friday. It was on the kids' channel and it got some great reviews. Would you like to come with me to the TV studio on Saturday? — **Yes – ask what time.**

Dad says he can give you a lift or you and your mum can meet us there. Which do you prefer? — **Tell Tanya**

What shall we do after the show? It finishes at 8 pm. — **Suggest ...**

Write your email to Tanya, using all the notes.

Hi Tanya,

I watched a cool documentary about modern heroes and heroines. It was incredible! But it finished at midnight so I was really tired the next day at school.

I'd love to come with you to the studio. I'm free all day on Saturday. What time do they start filming the show?

I'm happy to get a lift with you and your dad. My mum also says we can get the underground so we can meet you at the studio. Why don't we go out for something to eat after the show? We both like that new Mexican restaurant.

Write soon, Katerina

2 **Which sentences in the reply from Katerina answer the notes on the email?**

____

____

____

3 **Add at least one other way to start and finish an email.**

Start	Finish	Sign your name
Hi Tanya,	Write soon,	Katerina

EXAM TIP! You should always put **your name** at the end of an email.

1 Complete the text. Use the words in the box.

had/got x3 built cut painted

My favourite celebrity moved into a castle a few weeks ago – the castle was very old so she **(1)** __________ a lot of things changed. She had all of the walls in her house **(2)** __________ gold and she **(3)** __________ thick red carpets put on all the floors. In the garden, she had a golf course and swimming pool **(4)** __________ – and she **(5)** __________ some of the plants **(6)** __________ to look like elephants!

2 Complete the sentences.

1 I read the review so I didn't watch the film.

If I __hadn't read__ the review, I would have __watched__ the film.

2 I didn't see my favourite singer at the shops so I didn't have a photo taken with him.

If I __________ my favourite singer at the shops, I would have __________ a photo taken with him.

3 I saw the interview, so I know that the celebrity has 20 dogs.

If I hadn't __________, I wouldn't have __________.

4 The hero lost his phone, so he didn't call the president.

If ______________________________

5 I saw the advert, so I bought a new computer.

____

3 Choose ten words from this unit. Record the words using the steps below.

Build your words

- Choose 10 words from this unit
- **Look it up**
  - In a dictionary
  - Online
  - In this book
- **Practice**
  - Write the definition
  - Write similar words
- **Show**
  - Write in a sentence
  - Say it to a friend

Mission in action!

- Present your scene.
- Watch and make notes.
- Vote for the best scenes!

Review ••• Units 7–9

1 **Watch the video and do the quiz.**

2 **Choose the correct words to complete the sentences.**

Tips for visiting our town

1 You **should** / **mustn't** ask about the opening hours at the tourist information centre.
2 You **mustn't** / **have to** have a picnic on the roundabout.
3 You **shouldn't** / **ought to** drop litter on the pavement.
4 You **mustn't** / **have to** bring a horse when you take the underground.
5 You **ought to** / **mustn't** buy your cinema tickets at the booking office.

3 **Complete the sentences.** Use *such … that* / *so … that.*

1 It was ________ a funny comedy ________ I woke my cat up because I laughed so loudly.
2 The cartoon was ________ long ________ I fell asleep before it finished.
3 The action film was ________ exciting ________ I told my friends to see it too.
4 The questions on the quiz show were ________ easy ________ I only got one wrong.
5 On Thursday, I watched a film. It was ________ a terrifying horror film ________ I couldn't sleep.
6 It was ________ an interesting documentary ________ I watched it twice.

4 **Find the mistakes.** **Write the correct sentences.**

1 When we were children we use to go on holiday together.

____

2 I used to buying postcards from every place I went to on holiday.

____

3 In the past people were poor and they used to living in small houses.

____

4 The cinema is in town where we use to go every weekend.

____

5 I used to cycling in the countryside every day.

____

5 **A health expert is coming to your school. Say the questions as indirect questions.**

Please could you tell me … ? Do you know … ?
Would you mind explaining … ?

6 **In pairs, talk about what the town has had done.**

They've had the sculpture cleaned.

7 **Complete the texts.**

A

(1) __________ I found $250 million, I'd be amazed. First I'd go shopping, then I'd get some presents for my family. I think my dad (2) __________ like a helicopter!

B

If my rabbit could talk, I'd like to know what its favourite foods are. I think he likes carrots, but perhaps he prefers cake! (1) __________ also like to know (2) __________ he likes living with me, or if he'd prefer to live in the wild.

C

If I was a fruit, (1) __________ be a coconut because I'm very relaxed. I'd love to live somewhere warm – a beach would be great, too. I (2) __________ like it if people tried to eat me though!

8 **Complete the sentences (A–D).**

A If I was three metres tall __________

B If I found $250 million behind my sofa __________

C If my rabbit could talk __________

D If I could live anywhere in the world __________

9 **Choose and complete two of the challenges.**

CHALLENGE 1

Think of a feeling or emotion that starts with each of the following letters:

B-R-A-I-N M-A-P-S

CHALLENGE 2

Look at Unit 8 pages 93 and 96. What are five things that the place you live has got? What are five things that the place you live hasn't got?

CHALLENGE 3

Look at Unit 9. Find:

- three exciting kinds of TV programme.
- two funny kinds of TV programme.
- three kinds of TV programme where you learn new things.

Pronunciation

Unit 1 Plural pronunciation of 's'

3 1.04 **Listen and repeat.** Then listen again and write the words.

/z/	/s/
days	

Unit 2 Syllabus stress in two-syllable words

4 1.17 **Listen and repeat.** Then listen again and underline the stress in each word.

1 laptop
2 keyboard
3 software
4 handbag
5 raincoat
6 hardware
7 printer
8 program
9 tracksuit
10 costume

Unit 3 Contracted forms

1 1.26 **Listen and repeat.** Then listen again, which verb form do you hear?

1 shouldn't should
2 can can't
3 wouldn't would

Unit 4 Sentence stress

1 2.05 **Listen and repeat.** Then listen again and underline the stressed words.

1 How long have you been ill?
2 I've been ill for a while.
3 How long have you had a fever?
4 I've had it since last week.

Unit 5 Verb endings in the past

1 2.18 **Listen and repeat.** Then listen again and write the words in the correct column.

/id/	/t/	/d/
planted	cooked	rained

Unit 6 Schwa

1 2.25 **Listen and repeat. Then tick the words or phrases with unstressed syllables.**

1 dishwasher
2 the dishwasher
3 The dishwasher is in the kitchen.
4 curtains
5 the curtains
6 We've had the curtains for a long time.

2 2.26 **Listen again. Underline the unstressed syllables.**

Unit 7 /b/ /v/ /w/

3 3.03 **Listen and repeat.** Then write the words in the correct column.

/v/	/b/	/w/
positive		

Unit 8 Intonation in questions

1 3.15 **Listen and repeat.** Which questions are pronounced politely?

Unit 9 Word stress

3 3.21 **Listen and repeat.** Then underline the stressed syllables.

1 cartoon
2 action
3 broccoli
4 amazed
5 sightseeing
6 gallery
7 soap opera
8 embarrassed
9 onion
10 accident

Grammar look!

UNIT 1 Comparative adjectives, adverbs and *as … as*

For short adjectives ending in a vowel + a consonant, double the last letter and add *-er.*

big > bigger

*My raincoat is **bigger than** my jeans.*

For short adjectives ending in *-e*, add *r.*

large > larger

*Canada is **larger than** India.*

For two syllable adjectives ending in *-y*, change the *y* to *i* and add *-er.*

heavy > heavier

*Elephants are **heavier** than crocodiles.*

For longer adjectives put *more/less*, in front of the adjective.

important > **more/less** exciting

*Swimming is **more exciting than** tennis.*

(not) as … as …

We can use *(not) as … as …* to say something is (not) the same.

*My brother is **not as tall as** me.*

*My hair is **not as long as** my sister's.*

Practice

1 Complete the sentences.

1 My shoes are __________ __________ my brothers! (big)

2 Maths is __________ __________ __________ science. (difficult)

3 The Statue of Liberty isn't __________ __________ __________ the Empire State Building. (tall)

4 The heart of a blue whale is __________ __________ __________ a polar bear. (heavy)

5 This programme about dinosaurs is __________ __________ the one about penguins. (bad)

6 My pet snake is __________ to my bed __________ the kitchen. (close)

UNIT 1 The present simple with future meaning

We use the present simple to talk about events that are part of a future plan or timetable.

*The train **leaves** at 8 am.*

*The test **is** on Tuesday next week.*

*What time **do** you land?*

Practice

1 Complete the sentences. Use the correct form of the words in the box.

be leave start go

1 Hurry up! The film __________ in ten minutes.

2 Our train __________ at 10:45 am tomorrow.

3 She __________ to Spain in June on holiday.

4 The maths test __________ next Thursday.

UNIT 2 The zero and first conditional

We use conditional sentences to talk about possible situations or actions and their results. They have two clauses: an *if*-clause and a main clause.

We use the first conditional to talk about things which we think will happen.

We use the zero conditional to talk about things which are always true.

	***If* clause**	**Main clause**
First conditional:	*If we go by bus,*	*we'll get there late.*
Zero conditional:	*If my laptop doesn't work,*	*I ask my dad.*

Practice

1 **Match the sentence halves.**

1 If I get home soon, …
2 If my team wins the match, …
3 If you put money in the machine, …
4 If my sister forgets her homework again, …
5 If my dad's computer goes wrong, …

a you hear music.
b her teacher will be really angry.
c I'll have a party at my house!
d I'll call you.
e he sits with his head in his hands.

UNIT 3 The passive (present simple)

We form passive verbs with the correct tense of the verb *be* + past participle. We use passive verbs when we don't know who does something or when we don't need to know who did something.

To say who did something, we use the passive + *by* + the person or thing.

*Maths **is taught** in all schools.* (They teach maths in all schools.)

*Cricket **is** usually **played** in the summer.*

*Maths **is taught by** Mr Little.*

Practice

1 **Complete the sentences. Use the words in brackets and the present simple passive.**

1 A lot of tea __________ in China. (grow)
2 Millions of bottles of water__________ every day. (sell
3 Loud music __________ here every night. (play)
4 Our furniture __________ out of wood. (make)
5 Thousands of phones __________ every day. (lose)
6 I __________ on Fridays. (pay)

Unit 3 Modal verbs

We use *can/can't* or *could/couldn't* + infinitive without *to* to talk about ability or inability.

To talk about the past we use *could*.

***Can** Anna speak French? No, she **can't** but she **can** speak Chinese.*

*Max **could** walk when he was one, but he **couldn't** talk until he was two.*

***Could** he talk when he was one? No, he **couldn't**.*

We use *may*, *might* + infinitive without *to* to talk about something when we are not sure.

*It **may** be sunny tomorrow.*

*We **might** not go to Jack's party at the weekend.*

We can use *might*, *may* and *could* to talk about possibilities in the present or the future. But we can only use *can* to talk about possibilities in the present.

*It **might** be very hot tomorrow.*

*We **may** go swimming this afternoon.*

*There **could** be a storm later this evening.*

*It **can** snow here in April, but it doesn't often happen.*

The form of these verbs never changes. For example, we cannot say: *He cans. / They mighted.*

We use the question forms *May I …* or *Could I …* to ask for permission, not to talk about possibilities.

We rarely use the short forms *mayn't* or *mightn't*.

We often use *would* to make requests. It's a more polite and indirect form of *will*.

***Would** you like to play golf?*

We often use *would* (or the contracted form *'d*) in the main clause of a conditional sentence when we talk about imagined situations.

*He **wouldn't** like it if you wore his helmet.*

We use *shall I* and *shall we* to make offers and suggestions, and to ask for advice.

***Shall** I get you some medicine?*

The negative form of *shall* is *shan't*. We don't use *don't, doesn't, didn't* with *shall*.

*I **shan't** be home tomorrow night.*

Practice

1 Complete sentences with *can('t)*, *could(n't)*, *may*, *might*, *would* or *shall*. Sometimes more than one answer is possible.

1 I've looked everywhere for my mobile, but I __________ find it.

2 My brother __________ swim when he was less than a year old.

3 I'm not sure what to do tonight. I __________ go to Jo's party.

4 __________ I put this here?

5 Polly isn't looking very well. I think she __________ have flu.

6 I __________ play the piano really well.

7 __________ you like to come to the cinema with me?

8 Kieran __________ ride a bike until he was 12.

Unit 4 The present perfect with *how long*, *for* and *since*.

We use the present perfect to talk about something that started in the past and continues into the present.

Use the present perfect with *for* to talk about a period of time

***I've studied** English **for** six years. **We've lived** in Berlin **for** three months.*

Use the present perfect with *since* to talk about points in time or when something began.

***I've studied** English **since** 2015. **We've lived** in Berlin **since** June.*

We use ***How long …?*** to ask about the duration of a state or activity.

A ***How long** have you **been** ill?*

B Since yesterday.

Practice

1 Choose the correct words to complete the sentences.

1 I haven't seen my sister for **last weekend / two weeks.**

2 My parents have been married for **1999 / 14 years.**

3 I haven't done any homework since **last weekend / two weeks.**

4 I've had my bike since **January / six months.**

5 My father has worked as a doctor for 23 **years ago / years.**

6 Juan has played the guitar since **the age of nine / seven years.**

Unit 4 The present continuous for future plans

We can use the present continuous to talk about the future. It shows that we have already decided something and usually that we have already made a plan or arrangements.

***I'm seeing** Alice on Saturday.*

***He's** not **going** to the match.*

***We're leaving** in the morning.*

Spelling *-ing* forms

Most verbs: add *-ing* to the infinitive (*watching/finding*)

Verbs ending in *-e*: take off *-e* and add *-ing* (*liking/writing*)

Verbs ending in one vowel and one consonant: repeat the last consonant and add *-ing* (*putting/running*)

Practice

1 Read the sentences and say 'future' or 'now'.

1 We're seeing that new film tomorrow. I bought the tickets online.
2 He's going on holiday on Tuesday.
3 I'm doing this project at the moment so I can't chat.
4 She's not listening to me.
5 They're moving house next Thursday.
6 Are you watching this?

Unit 5 *Rather* and *prefer*

We use *prefer* to say we like one thing or activity more than another. We can use a prepositional phrase with *to* when we compare two things or actions.

*I **prefer** tea **to** coffee.*

*We **prefer** going by ferry **to** flying.*

We use *would prefer* or *'d prefer*, followed by the infinitive with *to* or a noun, to talk about present and future preferences.

***I'd prefer to go** swimming.*

***Would** you **prefer chicken** or **lamb**?*

*She**'d prefer not to drive** at night.*

We use *would rather* or *'d rather* followed by the infinitive without *to*, to talk about preferring one thing to another.

***I'd rather stay** at home tonight.*

***Would** you **rather play** rugby or football?*

Practice

1 Use one phrase from each box to make sentences.

I'd rather	stay at home tonight.
She'd prefer	salmon to steak.
Would you prefer	to drive or catch the train?
I prefer	swimming to running.
Would you rather	watch a film or go for pizza?
He prefers	walking to school to cycling.

Unit 5 The passive (past simple)

We form the passive by using a form of the verb *be* followed by the past participle of the main verb.

*Our school **was built** in 2012.*

We use the passive …

- when we are more interested in who or what is affected by the action.

  *My car **was made** in France.* (I am more interested in my car than workers or the company that made it.)
- if we don't know who did the action.

  *My bike **was stolen** yesterday.* (I don't know who stole it.)
- when who or what did something is obvious, so doesn't need saying.

  *The driver of the car **was arrested**.* (We know that the police arrest people so we don't need to say this.)

To say who or what did the action in a passive sentence we can add a *by* phrase (this thing or person is called the agent).

*This opera **was composed by** Mozart.* (Mozart is the agent.)

Practice

1 Complete the sentences. Use the words in the brackets and the present or past passive.

1 Last year's final, ________ (play) in the new stadium and ________ (watch) by over two million people.
2 I ________ (give) a new watch for my birthday.
3 Our house ________ (build) twenty years ago.
4 Our rubbish ________ (collect) once a week. Some of it ________ (recycle) but the rest ________ (take) to a special site outside the town.

Unit 6 *a lot of, lots of, a few, a little, many, much*

These words and phrases are quantifiers. They tell us how much or how little of something there is.

For small quantities use …

- *a few* with plural countable nouns.

  ***A few** people in my class speak Russian.*

- *a little* with uncountable nouns.

  *I'd like **a little** advice about going to university, please.*

For large quantities use …

- *many* with plural countable nouns.

  *There aren't **many** trains at night.*

  *How **many** times have you been to London?*

- *much* with uncountable nouns in questions and negative sentences.

  *How **much** money do you need?*

  *We don't have **much** time.*

- *a lot of* or *lots of* with plural countable nouns or uncountable nouns.

  ***A lot**/**lots of** students ride bikes to college.*

  *You can save **a lot**/**lots of** money if you cycle or walk.*

Practice

1 Correct the sentences.

1 We haven't got many time. Let's hurry.

____

2 I drink a few water as soon as I wake up.

____

3 There are a lot things we need to discuss.

____

4 There isn't many traffic in town.

____

5 I've only got little money.

____

6 How much pairs of shoes have you got?

____

Unit 6 Tag questions

Tags are either questions, statements or imperatives added to a clause to invite a response from the listener.

Tags consist of one of the auxiliary verbs *be*, *do* or *have* or a modal verb, plus a subject, which is most commonly a pronoun.

When we use the auxiliaries *be*, *do* or *have* or a modal verb in the main clause, this verb is used in the tag.

If there is no auxiliary or modal verb in the main clause, we use *do*, *does*, *did* in the tag.

Main clause	*be, do, have,* modal	Subject pronoun
He's cooking dinner,	isn't	he?
She plays hockey,	doesn't	she?
You can't sing,	can	you?
They dance well,	don't	they?
We can stay here,	can't	we?
She's been to Italy,	hasn't	she?

Practice

1 Write the tag questions.

1 The shops don't open until 9:30, __________ ?

2 You can ride a bike, __________ ?

3 Tony plays the guitar well, __________ ?

4 You haven't seen Mum, __________ ?

5 She's very clever, __________ ?

6 You can't see my mobile phone, __________ ?

7 They aren't very quiet, __________ ?

Unit 7 *needn't, have to, should, ought to, must, mustn't*

needn't

We use *need* mostly in the negative form to say that there is no necessity to do something. We form the negative by adding *not* after *need*. *Need not* can be contracted to *needn't*.

You ***needn't*** *take off your shoes.*

have to

We use *have/has to* + infinitive to talk about things that we need to do.

We ***have to*** *go to school five days a week.*

We use *don't have/doesn't have to* + infinitive to talk about things that we do not need to do.

We ***don't have to*** *go to school at the weekend.*

should and *ought to*

Should and *ought to* have similar meanings and uses. *Ought to* is more formal and less common than *should*.

We use *should* to talk about what is the best thing to do in a situation. We often use *should* to give advice.

We use the infinitive without *to* with *should* but *ought* is followed by *to*.

There ***should*** *be four candles on the cake.*

There ***ought to*** *be four candles on the cake.*

He ***shouldn't shout*** *so loudly.*

must/mustn't

Use *must/mustn't* + infinitive without *to* …

- to talk about rules.

  We ***must be*** *at school by 8:30 every morning.*
- to give strong advice.

  You ***must be*** *careful when you cross the road.*
  You ***mustn't cross*** *without looking.*

Must does not change its form.

We do not use *must* in questions. We use *have to*.

Do you ***have to*** *wear uniform for school?*

There is no simple past form of *must*. We use *had to*.

We ***had to*** *be at school at 7:30 yesterday.*

Practice

1 Complete the sentences with *need(n't), (don't) have to, should(n't), ought to* or *must(n't)*.

1. I ________ do any homework tonight.
2. Students ________ be late to school.
3. We ________ hurry – there's lots of time.
4. You ________ to wear your coat – it's cold.
5. You ________ switch your mobile off in class.
6. I ________ practise my guitar every day.
7. I ________ to have my hair cut.

Unit 7 *such … that/so … that*

We use *so* and *such* as intensifiers to mean 'very, very'.

It was ***so*** *dark (****that****) we could hardly see.*

We don't use *so* before an adjective + a noun. We use *such*.

She took ***such a lovely photo*** *of my dog* ***that*** *I cried.*

Not ~~She took so a lovely photo of my dog that I cried.~~

Practice

1 Match the sentence halves.

1	It was such a …	A	that I couldn't go to the doctor.
2	It was such …	B	that I'm sure he'll do well.
3	I was so ill …	C	hot chilli that I couldn't eat it.
4	She was so embarrassed …	D	a bad storm that the tree fell down.
5	He is such a good student …	E	that she hid her face.

Unit 8 Indirect questions

Indirect questions are a polite way of asking for information.

Direct questions	Indirect questions
Are you busy later?	Could you tell me if you're busy later?
Do you know the time?	I was wondering if you know the time.
Where do you work?	I'd like to know where you work.
When did we last meet?	I can't remember when we last met.

The word order in indirect questions is the same as for sentences. We do not use auxiliary verbs *do, does* or *did*.

If there is no question word (*what, when* etc.), use *if* or *whether.*

In indirect questions the tense does not change.

Practice

1 Rewrite the questions as indirect questions. Start with the phrase in brackets.

1 Where do you live? (Could you tell me …)

2 Are you doing anything at the weekend? (I was wondering …)

3 What did we do last weekend? (I can't remember …)

4 What did you think of the film? (I'd like to know …)

Unit 8 *Used to / didn't use to*

Affirmative / Negative forms

I/you/he/she/ it/we/they	used to didn't use to	enjoy watching football.

Question forms

Did	I/you/he/she/ it/we/they	use to	play football?

We use *used to* + the infinitive to talk about …

- things that happened regularly in the past but don't happen now.

  *I **used to drink** tea for breakfast, but now I always drink coffee.*
- actions that didn't happen in the past, but happen now.

  *I **didn't use to drink** coffee, but now I have three cups a day.*
- past states or conditions that are no longer true.

  *I **used to have** long dark hair.*
  *I **didn't use to** like jazz.*

In the negative and question forms, the spelling is *use* not *used.*

Used to only refers to the past. There is no present form.

Practice

1 Rewrite the sentences. Use the correct form of *used to*.

1 I like hot weather now, but I didn't in the past.

2 My brother played football regularly until he broke his leg.

3 My hair was black once.

4 Did you go on holiday with your parents when you were a child?

5 When I was younger, I didn't get up late.

Unit 9 Causative *have/get*

We use *have something done* to talk about things we ask other people to do for us, things that we do not want to, or cannot, do ourselves.

Get something done has the same meaning but is more informal.

*I'm **getting my hair cut** tomorrow.*

The order of words is *have* + object + past participle. The incorrect word order changes the meaning.

*She **has** her **hair cut**.* (Someone does it for her.)

*She **has cut** her **hair**.* (She did it herself.)

We can use *have something done* in any tense.

*I (don't) **have** my hair **cut** every week.*

*We're (not) **having** our flat **decorated**.*

*We **had** (didn't have) our computer **repaired** yesterday.*

*We'll (We won't) **have** our **car washed** tomorrow.*

*We should **have** our **broken** window **mended**.*

*Have you **had** your jacket **cleaned** recently?*

Practice

1 Put the words in order.

1 you / your / had / cut / hair?
Have you had your hair cut?

2 bedroom / have / painted / might / my / blue
I ______

3 fixed / had / Michael / yet? / bike / his
Has ______

4 get / teeth / every / my / months / polished / six
I ______

5 checked / your / computer / have / viruses / should / for
You ______

Unit 9 The second conditional

We use the second conditional to talk about unlikely situations/actions. We can also use it to imagine things.

If clauses can come before or after the result clause but if the *if* clause comes before the result clause, it is followed by a comma.

We can use *were* instead of *was* in second conditional *if* clauses.

***If* clause: *If* + past verb**	**Result clause: *would* + infinitive**
***If** we **went** by bike,*	*we**'d get** there very late.*
***If** I **were/was** you,*	*I**'d look** for a new hobby.*

OR

*We**'d get** there very late **if** we **went** by bike.*

*I**'d look** for a new hobby **if** I **were** you.*

Practice

1 Write second conditional sentences.

1 I'd like to play basketball but I'm not very tall.
If I were/was taller, I'd play basketball.

2 She can't get a job in Canada because she doesn't speak English.
______

3 I haven't got enough free time to learn to play a musical instrument.
______

4 I want to send Tom a message but I don't know his email address.
______

5 My uncle's too old to be an airline pilot.
______

6 I don't read very quickly because my eyesight isn't very good.
______

7 I'd like to buy a Mercedes car, but I haven't got enough money.
______